MW01352236

I Only Look This Good Because My "Genes" Fit So Well

by

Lee Anne Marlett Evans

authorHOUSE™
1663 Liberty Drive, Suite 200
Bloomington, Indiana 47403
(800) 839-8640
www.AuthorHouse.com

This book is a work of non-fiction. Unless otherwise noted, the author and the publisher make no explicit guarantees as to the accuracy of the information contained in this book and in some cases, names of people and places have been altered to protect their privacy.

First published by AuthorHouse 06/14/05

ISBN: 1-4208-3313-8 (sc)

Library of Congress Control Number: 2005904244

Printed in the United States of America
Bloomington, Indiana

This book is printed on acid-free paper.

Acknowledgements

No undertaking is ever completed without much assistance and support from others. A simple "thank you" seems so inadequate considering the magnitude of the contributions from the following people.

To the staff of Author House, particularly Ron Boles who smoothed my ruffled feathers just in time. I was ready to pull them out completely...

To Peter Branum, Executive Director, Museum of East Alabama for your interest and encouragement...

To Albert Killian, LTC (retired) for confirming my belief that George Marlett is important to more people than just his children...

To Tom Oscar for being such a good friend...

To my siblings, Peggy Roudabush, Pat Rushton, Cathy Ponder, and Rusty Marlett. How empty (and boring) my life would have been without you...

To my children, Drew, Dan, Bart and Matt for always telling me I'm the coolest momma in the world and that they don't believe there is anything I can't do...

To Cathy Ponder and my brother-in-law, Mike (Mac). I'm so thankful God looked ahead and simplified my life by combining my sister and my best friend and editor extraordinaire into one person...

And, saving the best for last...to my husband, Bobby Evans, for his love, patience, and understanding (as much as any man can understand any woman!)...

A sincere, but not simple, "Thank you!"

Dedication

In memory of
Maxine Mann Marlett
Oct 7, 1922 - Oct 12, 2002

Table of Contents

Forward

From Albert F. Killian, LTC (Retired) ANG

Two softball-related events capture both the personality and character of George (Red) Marlett. Both give insight into his determination always to do his best.

The following selection from the *Opelika Daily News* tells of a game played between the Opelika Prisoner of War Camp team and a team from Shawmut, Alabama. It is an example of Red's determination, even in a softball game.

> Robertson, left fielder for Shawmut, came to bat and at the very first pitch across the plate he swings with all his might. The ball traveled high and far, and as fast as the ball traveled, Sgt. Marlett, left fielder for the Camp team traveled just as fast. Far into left field and into the high grass went Marlett, through weeds, splashing through water, reached above his head and pulled the ball down. The game continued with the Camp team scoring in every inning.

A second incident took place during Alabama National Guard summer camp at Ft. McClellan, Alabama. The National Guard team needed to play and win one more game in order to win the league championship. However, before the final game they were required to be on maneuvers at Ft. McClellan. A no-show would forfeit the game and the title. Red made the decision; he was determined they would play the game. At the end of training day, the team loaded up a duce-and-a-half truck. Changing into softball uniforms in route, they drove back to Opelika arriving just in time for the final game. The team went immediately onto the field from the truck. Due to Red's decision, the team won the game and championship. No time for celebration, though; they drove back to Ft. McClellan, had a brief rest and performed their assigned duties the next day.

During Red's tenure in the US Army and Alabama National Guard, he was just as determined to do his best. His character and integrity can be summarized in one sentence: "After Red's service as First Sergeant, he became the gauge by which all other first sergeants were measured." All those I knew came up short. The Alabama National Guard will never again see the likes of 1st Sgt. George (Red) Marlett.

Chapter 1
The "D" in DNA stands for "Daddy"

I pretty much always considered Daddy my hero. He was big and strong, could fix anything that was broken, find anything that was lost, and cook anything on the grill and on and on. He was a patriot – not a typical southern democrat; but he was a strong supporter of Governor George Wallace who is remembered most for his stand on desegregation. Daddy was a soldier, the best home-run hitter in Opelika Parks and Recreation Softball League, the telephone man who could climb poles faster than anybody else. To me, there was nothing he could not do. Not until Tom Brokaw wrote so beautifully about The Greatest Generation did I fully understand who this man was. My daddy was part of that greatest generation.

Like most Christian believers I can easily recall difficult circumstances in my life and relate them to the promises God has made to always be directly involved in my life. Jeremiah 1:5 *"Before I formed you in the womb, I knew you..."*(New American Standard Translation) has always meant to me that God was with me from the time of conception rather than at the moment of my birth. However, in my preparations and in gathering information for this book, I've come to realize that God was in my life many, many years before I was even a possibility.

- Having a better understanding of those men and women among The Greatest Generation helped me know better who Daddy is. Yet the more I learn about him, the more I realize that he did not just become who he is as a result of World War II. There were people who influenced his life as a young boy, both positively and negatively; people whose time on Earth was over long before mine ever began. Just as they had a hand in shaping his life, someone else had helped shape their lives, and so on.

As I meditate on this idea, another of my favorite scriptures comes to mind and also takes on a deeper meaning than ever before. Jeremiah 29:11 *"I know the plans I have for you, declares the Lord, plans for welfare and not calamity, to give you a future and a hope."* (New American Standard Translation) I believe that in preparation for our success God strategically places the players in our lives many generations before we arrive.

It is my hope and prayer, that you will reflect on your own life and, perhaps, take the opportunity to thank God for it. If possible, also thank those who have played a role either directly or indirectly in you becoming who you are.

George Joseph Marlett was born November 17, 1921 in a small coal mining town in Pennsylvania. The following chapter, told in first person, relates some of the childhood memories he has lovingly shared with his children.

Chapter 2
Daddy's Memoirs

LITTLE BOY ALONE

I can't remember my parents ever living together; my mother left me to be raised by her parents. At the time her brother, Ed, and sister, Martha (whom I called Marcie) were still living at home and going to school. We all lived in the coal mining village of Tipperary, Pennsylvania. I loved Aunt Marcie and followed her everywhere I could. She was the one who really looked after me more than anybody else when I was a little boy.

My grandfather worked in the mine there. During the summer my Uncle Ed worked there, too. At the end of one summer we moved to another mining town called Frog Hollow. I went with Grandpa and Uncle Ed to get their tools from the mine in Tipperary. It was the first, and almost the last, time I would be in a mine. As we gathered their tools and started making our way out of the mine, we stopped about four miles from the entrance to rest. Not having ever seen inside of a mine before, I didn't recognize the electrical wire that powered the motor to pull the coal cars. I had been carrying a copper needle used to tamp black powder into a one-inch hole to blast the coal down. I put the needle on the ground next to that 440-volt power wire and nearly scared Grandpa and Uncle Ed to death. That was when I got my first lesson in respecting the power of electricity. One inch closer to the power wire and my life's story would have ended right here!

The next morning Grandpa went to work in the mine at Frog Hollow while the rest of us moved our household furnishings from Tipperary. At the end of the day, I went to the mine to meet him and lead him to our new house. Grandma had supper ready when we got back. After Grandpa finished eating, he asked where the outhouse was. Grandma pointed to the back porch where our new "modern convenience" was located. He hesitated, but went inside the in-door bathroom. In a little while he came back to the kitchen and said, "Don't unpack anything; we're not staying here. I will not live in a house where you eat and do your outhouse business in the same place." Grandma finally convinced him that all the company houses were built like that. He eventually agreed to stay and we lived there several years. I remember Aunt Marcie starting me in first grade while we lived in Frog Hollow.

The following summer Aunt Marcie had a baby girl; she named her Janie. They lived with us since Aunt Marcie and Janie's daddy were not married. It was my job to push Janie's cradle and rock her to sleep. A lot of times I wanted to go and do something else; maybe Aunt Marcie was trying to pay me back for always following her around. I might have fussed about having to push Janie's cradle, but I would have done just about anything for Aunt Marcie.

After Aunt Marcie and Janie's daddy, Leo, got married, we moved to Fiddlersgreen. I certainly did miss her. With Aunt Marcie gone, Uncle Ed sort of saw himself as being in charge of me. By then he worked in the mine full time and didn't go to school any more. I was happiest when he was at work. He whipped me a lot; sometimes it seemed like for no reason at all.

Grandpa came into a little bit of money from some place and bought a car with it. A few days later, Uncle Ed broke his arm turning the crank on the car. I sure hated that because he couldn't do his job at the mine and I knew he'd still be able to dish out my punishment with one arm. But just a few days after that, I was relieved when he tried to turn the crank on the car with his other hand and broke that arm, too. I was glad, but, of course, I kept my jubilation to myself.

OLD FASHIONED REMEDIES

I guess I had just gotten so accustomed to being hurt and marked up that I took up where Uncle Ed left off. During the time his arms were broken and he couldn't hit me, I nearly cut off my own toe. Grandma lined it up straight and soaked it in kerosene oil, and then she wrapped it up real tight. It sticks out at a funny angle now, but at least it grew back together and stayed on my foot.

Another time, I was rolling down a grassy hill because I didn't have anything better to and that hill was pretty fun to roll down. It was really steep with a creek running along at the bottom of it. To keep myself from rolling into the creek, I stuck my hand out to stop myself. I never saw the broken fruit jar there and cut my hand up terribly. Again, Grandma soaked it in kerosene oil and wrapped it up. It healed really well and stayed attached, too, but I have a big scar to remind me of that day.

GRANDMA'S JUSTICE

My grandma had some old-fashioned ways about her, but I suppose if it had not been for her I never would have gotten grown. She was a funny old lady with some peculiar ways about her. When she made her mind up about something, she wouldn't hardly change it – even when she knew she was wrong.

Grandma had a clothes wringer and let the woman next door borrow it. When the lady finished her laundry and brought it back, Grandma insisted the one she returned was not the one she had loaned her. When the neighbor disagreed, Grandma had her arrested. They couldn't resolve their differences and the day came around for the case to be heard in court.

We lived about a half mile from the judge's office and had to walk there because Grandpa was at work. Uncle Ed didn't have another arm to break and Grandma couldn't crank the car. It wouldn't have mattered since she didn't know how to drive the thing any way. I had to carry that heavy wringer to the judge's office and sit there all day holding it on my lap because Grandma was afraid somebody might steal it if I put it down. The judge did not get around to hearing her case that day and I had to carry that thing all the way back home again. She never did go back to court over it; I don't exactly remember what happened about the case. I think Grandpa finally did convince her that it really was her clothes wringer. I was just happy I would not have to carry it back to town again.

One day Grandma got it into her head that Grandpa was sneaking around and seeing another woman who lived up the road from us. Both Grandma and Grandpa were known to drink a bit, and one night after a drinking spell, an argument broke out about that woman up the road. Grandpa didn't enjoy an argument as much as Grandma did so he just got up and left the house. Grandma kept drinking and stewing about his alleged indiscretions and decided that he must have gone up the road to see that woman. I watched as she went to the old trunk, took out our American flag that was kept there and wrapped it around her body. Then she headed up the road to beat up that woman for fooling around with Grandpa. She truly believed that woman could not hit her back as long as she was covered by the American flag. Not much came from the actual confrontation, but news of it traveled fast and resulted in a lot of talk around town.

SCOTCH WHISKEY

Every time the folks got to drinking – which was pretty often – the day would end with a lot of fussin' and cussin'. My grandpa was a Scotsman and came to the United States when he was a young man. Traditionally, his family in Scotland celebrated the New Year in a big way, and although he didn't live there any more, he still believed it should be the biggest holiday celebration of the year. He and all his sons (including Uncle Ed) would start drinking the Saturday before Christmas and continue to celebrate until the day after New Year's. Then it would take another week to get sober and fully recovered.

I always hoped Uncle Ed would drink enough to forget about what he thought was his duty to keep me in line. However, the drink seemed to only make him more conscious of me being wherever he didn't want me to be. No matter where I went, he would show up swearing he had told me not to be there, and would whip me all the way home. I sure did miss Aunt Marcie.

THE GREAT DEPRESSION

When I was eight years old we moved again so Grandpa could work in the mine at Purtain. One day when I was walking home from school, I saw Grandma and a lot of other people standing outside the entrance to Mine #6 where Grandpa worked. She told me that there had been a cave-in and some of the miners were hurt. Numerous people were working to get to the trapped miners and bring them out. Finally they brought Grandpa out; his back was broken, but we were so glad just to know he was alive. It was a while after they took him to the hospital before we knew that he would live. How much he would recover from his injuries was another question. While he was in the hospital we moved our belongings back to Fiddlers green.

But, Grandpa was a tough ol' bird and recovered enough to work again. It was 1929 and soon after returning to the mine, the Great Depression hit and all the mines shut down. There was no work for anyone. This was long before any government programs were available to help people when they were down and out.

Once a month a few men would be selected to go into the mines and inspect them. I didn't know what they inspected for, but I do know they didn't get paid for the day's work. They already owed the company rent for living in company houses. So what they would have made for a day's wage was just subtracted from the amount of rent owed. Just like many other folks, I went to bed hungry a lot of nights.

All the mules used to pull coal cars in the mine were brought out and turned loose in the fields to fend for themselves. People said the mules were better off than most families; they could at least eat the grass and survive. I was kind of envious of those mules sometimes. They didn't look happy, but they didn't look hungry either.

The mining company owned all the land around us, including the fields where the mules grazed. When the mules ate all the grass on the big field close to us, the company had it plowed up and gave each family a garden spot to use. I don't know where the seed came from but we planted a variety of vegetables including tomatoes and onions, cabbage and rutabagas, bush beans and pole beans, and corn. Every day I prayed for rain; I knew if it didn't rain, I would have to help Grandpa haul water in the evening from a lake about 200 yards from our garden. Every other morning we would go out early and cut brush to put around the plants to shade them from the sun.

If it had not been for those garden spots, I guess we, along with a lot of other people, would have just starved to death. All the banks were closed; so was the stock market. Even people who had been rather well to do before then lost every bit of what they had. Some even committed suicide over it. Whenever I think back on those days, I thank God for the blessings He poured out on us.

In 1932, I was eleven years old when Franklin D. Roosevelt was elected President of the United States. By the next year he had the economy on the upswing again and started the WPA and CCC Camps. The WPA built a road where we lived. Workers dug rock out of the mountains and broke them up into small pieces on the road. It looked like hard work as those men smashed those big rocks with sledge hammers. But people were so thankful to have work. The road bed was at least two feet deep so it would be below the frost line. Then the rock beds were covered with tar and gravel, so I guess that's where they got the name "tar roads." I'm sure the WPA did a lot of other things in communities, but I only remember them building roads.

The CCC Camps were for boys 12-18 years old. I personally think it was one of the best things that ever came to America. Boys would serve for six months and lived just like they do in the Army. They built their own camps, had their own cooks and constructed a lot of the state parks in our country which are still open and used today. I assume the workers were supervised by government employees, maybe military personnel. I know now that a lot of really good soldiers came out of those camps. They were paid $30 a month for their work; that was more money than anybody I knew had seen for a long, long time.

I wanted to go to the CCC Camp, but Grandpa thought of it as charity. Fortunately, he was one of the first men called back to work when the mine opened again. I wonder if he would have eventually given in and let me go to camp if he had not been recalled. Probably not; his pride would not have any part of us taking charity.

LIVING WITH DAD

I think my mother was living in Detroit when I was 12 years old; it had been a long time since I'd seen her. My father lived about twenty miles away from us in Dunlo. He heard about how Uncle Ed beat on me, so he came to find out why. After they talked awhile, he asked if I wanted to come live with him. To me, any place was better if Uncle Ed was not there, and I quickly agreed. It didn't matter that I knew nothing about where or how he lived. We walked the twenty miles from Fiddlers green to Dunlo, where I discovered my father lived in a house with his parents and my cousin Jean.

Jean's mother was my father's sister, Bertha. She had died some time back so I never knew her. I didn't know anything about Jean's father either, but it didn't take long to figure out that Grandmam did not like either one of us. I stayed as far away from her as I could; every time either Jean or I would get close to her, she would spit or hiss or strike out at us like a cat. Grandpap told us not to pay any attention to her, that she was crazy. He was sure right about that! Grandmam was as mean as any snake could ever be and she called us by terrible names instead of Jean or George. I thought she was a witch.

Grandpap was good to Jean and me. Poor Jean might not have survived after her mother died if Grandpap had not been there. But in the spring of 1934 Grandpap died. Since his family was Irish a big wake was in order. I remember helping dig his grave and then sitting up all night with seven or eight men at his wake. Each one of those men had his own jug of moonshine whiskey that they drank from all night long while they told stories about Grandpap. We buried him the very next day.

My Aunt Irene's husband had left her, so when Grandpap died, Aunt Irene and her children moved in with us. I was glad someone other than mean ol' Grandmam was there for Jean and me.

STEALING CORN

One night several of my buddies and I decided to have a corn roast. A man about a mile from town had a huge corn field and we figured he'd never miss a few ears. We built a good fire and after it got dark we went to steal five ears of corn a piece. The man must have seen our fire and had a pretty good idea what a bunch of boys like us had in mind, so he was watching his field. I had my five ears of corn and was anxious to get this feast underway when I heard my buddies hollering. They had been caught!

I took my five ears and headed for home slipping them into the house without anybody seeing me. The next day my grandmother cooked them for supper. My dad commented on how good the corn was and told Grandmam to get some more when she got a chance. She told him she didn't get the corn; she thought he brought it home. Well, he had heard about the cornfield incident at work so he knew right away that I was the one who got away. He looked at me and said, "We got a chore to tend to after supper." He had never whipped me, but I was sure he was about to. Instead, he and I walked to the farm where I stole the corn.

I was surprised to learn that he knew the man. They greeted each other, shook hands, and then my dad introduced us and said, "My boy's got something to tell you." I would have much rather had a beating than to tell that man I stole his corn and was the one who got away. But I did.

Dad told him that I brought the corn home and that we ate it before he knew it was stolen. He wanted to know how much he owed the man for it. The farmer said my confession was payment enough for him, but my dad didn't think so. He wanted to know what kind of punishment the other boys would have. The man said they were coming every day after school to harvest the whole field for him. Dad told him to expect me to be right there with them. It took us about two weeks to pick that whole field. When we finished, the man said we did a good job for him and gave each of us fifty cents. He said he hoped we learned a lesson from it. I can't speak for the others, but I definitely learned my lesson.

ALONE AGAIN

Not long after the cornfield fiasco, Dad lost his job and had to leave us to look for work. It was bad enough being around Grandmam after Grandpap died, but with my dad gone I had no intention of staying there with her. I ran away, the whole twenty miles back to Grandma and Grandpa's house in Fiddlersgreen. It was hard to decide between Grandmam and Uncle Ed.

When my mother moved back to Pennsylvania, she lived about a mile away in Portage. She was working for a family there keeping house and cooking for them. Sometimes I would go to see her and she would slip me something to eat.

She was a good cook and the people she worked for were nice folks.

But she left to work with another family about eight miles away. They were a nice family, too, and had a boy about my age. That was quite a walk for a little fellow, so I would go there on a Saturday and spend the night. I just wished they lived closer so I could go to see her more often.

FIGHTING ROOSTERS

Uncle Leo and Aunt Marcie had a car and sometimes would take us to see my Great-grandmother O'Hara. When I was a young teenager, Uncle Leo came to get us to go to his place for Thanksgiving. Grandpa said I couldn't go; he was raising some fighting roosters and said I had to stay home to keep the neighbor's rooster from fighting with ours through the fence. The neighbor man would not keep his big red rooster locked up. It ran loose and would come right up to our rooster's coop and try to fight. My job was to chase him away.

Before I could chase him off that day, the man came over and said, "Why don't you let your rooster out so they can fight?" I don't know why I thought that was just a good idea; maybe I thought they would get it out of their systems. Who knows? Since I knew where Grandpa kept the steel spurs our rooster fought with, I got them and put them on our little rooster.

I told our neighbor that our little guy could kill his big ol' rooster. He thought that was so funny and was laughing when I turned our rooster out of the coop. He was still laughing when our rooster made the first and last pass at his. Then our little champion just strutted like he was so proud of himself as he watched that big red rooster flop around on the ground. When our neighbor man stopped laughing and his rooster stopped flopping, our little rooster jumped up on top of his big red and crowed as loud as he could.

I didn't say a word. I just picked up our little guy, petted him a time or two, took off his spurs and put him back in his coop. It was obvious that our neighbor was really mad, so I didn't try to rub it in. I just washed the blood off the spurs and hung them back up in the house. It was good to know that I wouldn't have to chase off that neighboring rooster any more.

I sure didn't expect what came next. As soon as the folks drove up, that man came over and told Grandpa that I let our rooster out to kill his red rooster. He wanted Grandpa to pay him for his dead bird! Grandpa said ours couldn't have hurt his rooster because he didn't have any spurs on. When he found out the dual was over in one jump, though, Grandpa figured out what had happened. I got a terrible whipping and never let that rooster out again. But the more time that goes by and I think about that day, I've decided it was worth the whipping.

LITTLE PIG, LITTLE PIG

Uncle Ed finally married a woman he had been dating for several years. I think he married her because her family had money from a store they owned and from bootlegging moonshine. It really didn't matter to me as long as he didn't live with us any more and it would end my regular beatings.

I'm satisfied that Uncle Ed finally got what was coming to him, though, just before he left home. All the family was home getting ready to start the New Year celebration. Uncle Ed and Uncle Lou had been drinking all day and had a good size lead on the others. Grandma was raising a little pig for slaughter in the spring, but Uncle Ed and Uncle Lou decided there was no time like the present to kill the piglet.

They didn't care that Grandma had told them not to hurt it. They started boiling some water in the big black pot outside and said they were going to shoot the little pig anyway.

When I overheard them, I went into the house and got the shotgun; I told Grandma I was going to the woods and taking the gun with me. She didn't make any effort to stop me, so I hid just a little ways in the woods behind the house. I could still see and hear my drunk uncles fussing and cussing each other because they couldn't find the shotgun or me.

After more moonshine was consumed, they gave up on the gun and decided to just knock out the piglet with a hammer and cut his throat. They looked ridiculous trying to catch that pig and get it out of the pen. They were falling all over each other and the piglet, cussing each other and calling that little pig all kinds of ugly names. They did finally catch him, dragged him out upside down and fought with him until Uncle Ed had him trapped on the ground. Neither he nor the piglet could move. Hearing all the commotion without being able to see it, you would have thought they were wrestling a wildcat instead of a little bitty pig.

Uncle Lou got the pig turned over and caught between Uncle Ed's legs. Picking up that eight-pound hammer and raising it over his head almost caused him to loose his balance since he was already staggering from the booze. He let out a yell as he swung that hammer and I guess it scared that little pig. It squealed and wiggled right out from between Ed's legs. The momentum was in full force, though, as Uncle Lou brought that hammer down as hard as he could, hitting his brother square on the knee. As the piglet took off, Ed was rolling on the ground holding his knee and screaming at Lou. Uncle Lou's drunken state had caused him to follow the hammer's weight all the way to the ground, so he was rolling around, too, and cussing right back at Ed for letting the pig get away.

It was a sight to see, all right! Some of the others caught the little pig and put him back in the pen...til spring, any way. I was satisfied that it was a good day for both me and for the pig – definitely the best holiday I had ever experienced.

BECOMING A MAN

The summer that I was 14 was just about the best time of my life to that point. Uncle Leo bought a piece of land and planned to build a house on it for himself, Aunt Marcie and Janie. They wanted me to spend the summer helping build that house. I might have been a little jealous of Janie because she lived with her momma and daddy, but I didn't hold it against her at all. She was a sweet little girl as I recall.

I was so excited when summer break finally arrived and Uncle Leo came to get me. He was from a fine family and I loved him as much as I loved Aunt Marcie. His whole family was always very kind to me, and I was glad to find out his daddy and uncles would be helping build the house, too. They all worked hard and could work together without fighting with each other. That was something I didn't see much at home.

My first job for the house building was to help mix the mortar and carry it to the men who were laying the foundation. I don't mean to brag but I could keep mortar mixed and carried around to each of them before they ran out of the batch I brought before. I worked my scrawny little butt off to do it and was determined to do a good job for them.

At the end of the first day, Aunt Marcie and some of the ladies whose husbands were helping us fixed a big supper for us. It all looked so good and there was so much food. I had really worked up a big appetite; but it was the custom for the men to come to the table first and eat. I had washed my face and hands and was hanging out with the little kids waiting for our turn to eat. Uncle Leo's dad asked the blessing and then I heard him say, "Hey, where's our mortar man?" Aunt Marcie told him I was outside with the other children, and he said, "Well, go get him in here. Nobody eats until ALL the men are at the table."

He went on and on about how hard I hard worked that day and I deserved to eat with the rest of the men. Boy was I proud; that man's praise just made me want to work harder for them. He probably never knew how much his approval meant to me; praising me in front of everyone made it even more special. I'll never forget him for it; I felt like I grew up that day.

I stayed there with them the whole summer and we finished the house so they could move in before winter. I had to go back home, but I enjoyed every minute of every day that summer with Aunt Marcie and Uncle Leo.

That fall I learned how to drive a cut-down car that was made into a tractor. I drove that thing all around the back fields and along the back roads hauling apples on a farm where they made cider. I had to stay on the back roads because I was still only 14 and didn't have a driver's license. The work was not nearly as hard as building Aunt Marcie's house, but I had fun.

I was enrolled in school, but played hooky most of the time. Often I would just go fishing and take what I caught to my aunt's house. She would always cook them for me.

PAID TESTIMONY

My cousin rented a house in Solomon which belonged to the owners of the mine. It was situated back a ways out of town and any traffic back that far would have only been on mining business. No vehicle could go in or out without passing her house.

One morning I saw a truck go by toward the mine; I told my cousin that something just didn't seem quite right about it. She said I should watch for it coming back out and let her know which one it was. As it came back up the road, I saw that it was loaded with coal. My cousin knew the man driving, but she didn't think things seemed right either. The next day the mine owner came by and she mentioned it to him. Our suspicion was right; the man was arrested for trespassing and stealing the load of coal. Since my cousin and I were witnesses, we were told we would be called to testify in court.

There were quite a few miles between all those little mining towns but word traveled fast from one to the other. As soon as Grandpa heard about it, he sent word that if I got paid for testifying, I was not to spend any of the money because it was really his. Any money I had made working in the past I always had to give to him; that's just the way it was back then. Nobody earned much money so all of it went to take care of the family. Somehow, though, his thinking he had to remind me of that fact made me really resentful about it. Maybe it was because I knew he would spend some of it on whiskey.

I did get some money for testifying and I used it to buy myself a new jacket. I think that was the first brand new piece of clothing I had ever had, and did need it. But it was a long time before he stopped reminding me that I had stolen that money from him.

MY MENTOR, DEFENDER, PROTECTOR

One morning Grandma sent me to the store. She was aggravated because it was bread baking day and she was out of yeast. The store was quite a hike and I knew that every minute that went by meant she was losing valuable baking time. Normally I would stop off at the dam about halfway down the mountain and take a dive or two in the lake to cool off. But today I knew better than to make any stops. I needed to get back as fast as I could with that yeast so she could get started on the bread. Her fresh bread tasted so good.

As luck would have it, I could hear a truck coming up the lane behind me and decided to flag it down for a ride the rest of the way home. The driver and I started talking; he said his name was Ruben and that he was going over the mountain to pick up some props for the mine. Props were lengths of timber varying from two to six feet and used inside the mines to support the roof where coal had been taken out. Ruben had a regular agreement with the mining folks and made a little money for himself getting paid per piece for the props he delivered. It sounded interesting to me so I asked if I could tag along. When we got to the house he waited for me to take the yeast to Grandma and we headed over the mountain.

Ruben told me that he was divorced; his wife and three children lived in New York and he missed them very much. He had several little jobs like this one because he paid her a lot of alimony and child support. I could tell right off that he was an honest man and that it was important to him to always do the right thing. I knew he must be a person with a good reputation.

Ruben cautioned me about being really careful and to keep an accurate count as we loaded props on the truck. I spent all day with him as we made two trips over the mountain hauling props. It was hot that day and I got my hands full of splinters since I had no gloves to wear. But I didn't care. Ruben and I talked all day and I enjoyed every second of it. I hated for the day to end. I felt like we were becoming really good friends and that this would not be the last day we spent together.

I was glad that he seemed to take a liking to me as well. Just being around him taught me so much about life and being a man people could trust. He would even pay me a little money when he could. Though I was pleased to get it, the way he treated me was payment enough for helping him.

On Saturdays I would go to the garage Ruben's father owned to wash and grease his truck. Other than the mine props he would haul pulp wood to the mill, or haul coal from the mines to people's houses when they needed it. People paid him pretty good for that. My grandpa found out Ruben was paying me a little bit and, as usual, he wanted all the money I had made. We really fussed about that because I didn't have all the money I had been paid. By that time I was pretty much taking care of myself and not depending on them any more. I didn't feel like I owed him any money.

I told Ruben about the argument with my grandpa and he said that I probably shouldn't go with him any more. That just about broke my heart; Ruben had become more like a father to me than just a good friend. I said that I would slip around behind Grandpa's back to work with him if I had to. He didn't want me doing that, but saw how hurt I was and changed his mind. He said he probably couldn't pay me so much any more, though. As I said before, the way he treated me and the things he taught me were worth a whole lot more than a few dollars!

Ruben told me that he was planning a trip to New York soon because he missed his children and needed to see them. It made me feel a little sorry for myself; I wished so many times that at least one of my parents would miss me enough to come see me. But, at the same time, I realized that Ruben was a good man and that I was luckier than his own children since he spent time with me nearly every day. I was mighty thankful to know him.

The weekend that Ruben was away, I decided to go on to the garage and work on his hauling truck. While I was washing it a man came by looking for Ruben; he seemed kind of upset when I told him Ruben wouldn't be back until Monday. He told me that he had ordered a load of coal from the mine and expected it to have been delivered the day before but they never showed up with it. He was hoping Ruben would go get it for him. The weather was very cold and it was snowing; I knew the man's name was Mr. Stands and that he had little children at home. If Ruben had been there, I just knew he would have made sure that man had coal at his house before the day ended.

Even though I was not old enough to drive (legally, that is), I told Mr. Stands to get in and I'd get his coal for him. I had been hauling coal with Ruben long enough that I was pretty sure everybody I needed to deal with in the process knew me and was hoping they would let me haul it myself. Mr. Stands rode with me and I got his load of coal, took it to his house and unloaded it; he was sure grateful for it. I guess it was about a five-mile trip all together, but to me it seemed like a million miles. I was so relieved to get that truck back to the garage without anything bad happening to it.

But then the waiting until Monday when Ruben was due back felt like that whole truck of coal was weighing on my shoulders. Although I believed I had done the right thing like Ruben had taught me, I wasn't sure he would feel the same way. I was dreading Monday with every passing minute.

The rest of the weekend I tried to think of a way to tell him about it that would sound the best and keep me out of trouble. There must have been a million things that could have gone wrong and caused a disaster. But at the time I never thought about any of them. I just know how bad it would have been for the Stands family to go through the weekend with no heat. However I decided to break the news to Ruben of taking his truck without his permission, I'd be sure to remind him of that fact.

Monday finally came and I felt more weighted down than ever with what I knew I had to do. The great sounding speech I had prepared was gone from my head forever, mysteriously erased from my memory in my sleep, I guess. As I walked toward the garage I had no idea what I would say to Ruben. When I was close enough to see he was getting the truck ready for a full day of hauling, I called to him waving my hand trying to look like nothing was wrong. But my heart felt like a pounding hammer; I was so scared. Ruben looked up from his work, smiled at me and stuck his hand out for a shake with my hand. Then he slapped me on the back the way he always did. He told me he was glad to see me and I asked if he had a good visit with his kids and how they were doing. Then the conversation got really awkward and I knew it was time for my confession.

You can't imagine how surprised I was, and relieved, too, when Ruben spoke first and said, "Red Boy, Mr. Stands came by to see me last night when I got back in town. He told me what a mess he was in Saturday morning with no coal and that you just took care of it like a man for him. He said you did a great job and that you refused his pay. Well, he appreciated so much what you did for him that he wanted to be sure I knew about it, and he wanted to be sure you got this." He held out his hand to give me the same money Mr. Stands had offered me Saturday.

I still wasn't sure I should take the pay since I broke the law and used Ruben's truck without permission, even though what I did was good for that man and his family. I hesitated because I was still pretty surprised and speechless, too. Ruben took my hand, put the money in it, looked me right in the eye and said, "Thank you, Red Boy; I'm proud of you."

Hearing him say that must have made my head swell. I was so relieved, but I was also confused some about how he could be so proud of me. It just didn't make sense when he said I deserved to be paid for what I did when I broke the law doing it. We talked about that off and on just about all day. He taught me that life is just jammed full of decisions that are not easy and have an effect on people other than ourselves. Sometimes what you decide might not make much difference to you, or it might not be a good thing for you, but it might mean the difference in life and death for somebody else. He was able to think of one example after another all day to help me understand that better.

Then he went on to remind me how important it is for people to know you can be trusted. He asked me what I thought might have happened if Mr. Stands and I showed up at the mine to get his coal and someone there had known me to be dishonest in the past. I thought about it and said that probably Mr. Stands wouldn't have had any heat over the weekend. Ruben didn't say anything; he just grinned at me. It made me think I had said the wrong thing, so I asked him what was so funny. "I'm grinning," he said, "because you didn't even consider that they might have thought you had done something bad to me and stolen my truck. If they had, you might have been in jail until I got back to tell them what a good man you're growing up to be. I'm proud again that you thought first about somebody else rather than about yourself. You're a fine young man, Red Boy." My goodness, how that made my spirit soar. As soon as I turned sixteen, Ruben took me to get my driver's license and made me a legal driver.

There was a doctor who lived in town and had a big nice house with a beautiful yard. The doctor had ordered fifteen tons of coal and hired Ruben to deliver it for him. He said he wanted it unloaded into a bin in the basement, but that we could not drive over his grass to get it there. When we stopped at the garage to pick up a large canvas, I asked what we were going to do with it. Ruben said we would spread it down on the grass. I laughed and told him even if we drove over the canvas it would still mess up the man's grass! I was still laughing when Ruben said, "No, we'll spread it out, dump the coal on it, and we will shovel the load through the basement window to the coal bin." Now that was not so funny! But when we arrived with the first load and saw it was a lot closer from the driveway to the basement window than we thought, I felt better about it.

After we dumped the first load on the canvas I told Ruben to go ahead and get the next one; I would stay there and shovel while he was gone. That might save some time since it was probably going to take about four loads to fill the whole order. He agreed. When he got back with the second load, I had finished shoveling the first load and was waiting for him. He asked me who I hired to help shovel that load. I told him I didn't need anybody to help if he was going to be that slow every time. We both got a good laugh out of that. Every day working with Ruben was just getting better and better.

While I was shoveling the third load, going for three in a row having it all done before Ruben returned, the doctor came home. He got out of his car just cussing and yelling at me. Boy! He was furious because coal dust (not the coal, just the dust) had settled on the grass around the edges of the canvas. He kept asking me who told me to do that, and was my work always so messy. Didn't I have any respect for other people's property? He just kept screaming at me all the way into his house and wouldn't let me answer any of his questions.

That was the end of going three for three. I just stopped and walked down the driveway to wait by the side of the road for Ruben. He was back before too long and knew as soon as he saw me that something was wrong. He wanted to know what had happened, so I started telling him. Before I got very far, the doctor came down his driveway where I was sitting on the curb. Ruben got out of the truck and told me to get in. He just let the man yell until he got to the front of the truck. Then Ruben reached out, grabbed him, and slung him around to the side where I was sitting. Then he started yelling back at the man. He told him I was his boy, that he told me what to do and how to do it, that I always did a good job and nobody he could find could do it any better. He went on to tell him that we could have just dumped the whole fifteen tons in his driveway and told him to get it to his basement however he wanted. By the time Ruben finished with everything he had to say, the doctor was ready to apologize to me and to him. He asked us to finish the job and then paid me extra for shoveling the loads! Old Ruben sure had a gift for helping people see things his way.

Another day we were delivering coal to the VFW Club; Ruben went inside to collect for the hauling. By the time he finished with all the business stuff and came out again, I had al! the coal unloaded. He stopped at the door and motioned for me to come on inside. When I caught up to him at the door I could see Uncle Ed sitting at the bar; it was easy to tell he had been there drinking for a while. Not wanting any trouble, I just said, "I'll wait for you in the truck." Ruben knew how Ed had treated me most of my life and he put his hand on my shoulder and said, "Don't worry about Ed. He's not going to bother you." I was not nearly as sure of that as Ruben was, but I went on in with him anyway.

We were sitting at a table with some of Ruben's buddies when Ed saw me and yelled at me to get out of there. I started to get up and Ruben told me to sit back down. This whole situation was looking really bad and I didn't see any way it could get better. But, I was wrong. As Uncle Ed staggered over to our table threatening me all the way, Ruben stood up and told him, "Red is here with me and he'll leave with me when I'm ready to go. I'm not ready yet and I don't see anybody here that can make me leave until I am ready." Ed knew he didn't want to fight with Ruben; he wanted to fight with me. So he stuck his finger in my face and said something about waiting until I got home. It looked like this bad situation was getting worse for me by the minute until I heard Ruben say, “If you lay one hand on him later, I’ll find out about it and I’ll come kick your sorry a– all over Portage and back. And if you don’t get the h— out of here I might not wait until then. I’ll just do it now.”

The look on Ed’s face right then was almost as good as the day Uncle Lou hit him on the knee with the hammer. He left the club and I guess took the man at his word. He didn’t whip me then or ever again.

MARLETT IN THE MINE

After I turned sixteen years old, I didn’t get to see Ruben as much any more. Most young men just accepted the fact that when they got old enough they would start to work in the mine. I had not really planned to do that. Not because I didn’t want to, but because I didn’t have anybody to take me in. You couldn’t just apply for a job and get hired. Coal mining is a dangerous business and you had to work for at least two years as an apprentice to someone who had mining papers. That meant they had taken a test showing they were able to perform all the tasks like placing props to support the ceiling, use dynamite on the rock and blasting powder on the coal, laid the tracks for the mules to pull the cars, and other tasks.

Most miners took their sons in to train them when they were old enough. It was almost like a tradition handed down from father to son. Miners never worked alone; at least two men were required on a job, so that was another reason fathers usually trained their sons. The miner got paid for all the work the team did and the apprentice got paid for the odd numbered cars they filled. For example, if there were three cars of coal, the apprentice got paid for one and three;

if they filled five cars, he was paid for three of them. The miner was paid for all of them. So a father and son team could actually take home the whole payload. My dad was not around, my other uncles had their own sons to train, and I would not have worked with Uncle Ed anyway.

One my uncles knew a team that was about to break up because one of the miners was getting ready to bring his own son in. Since his partner had no son of his own to train, he brought me in and I worked with him. I was pretty fortunate to get in that way. My grandpa would have taken me in but by the time I was old enough, he was too old to work the coal. He mostly did just light maintenance work around the mine where it was not so strenuous or dangerous. He was really pleased that the tradition of Marletts in the mine would go on, even if I had to be trained by an outsider.

Coal mining was hard and dirty. You don't see much daylight because you go into the mine before the sun comes up and don't come out until after it has gone down. The only time we saw the sun was on Sundays, when the mine was closed. In the winter, if you weren't careful, the bright sun shining on the snow would almost blind you.

But mining was steady work. I got good pay for what I was doing; $15 every two weeks was more money than I had ever made. Grandpa let me keep fifty cents of it; $14.50 went to him to "help support the household."

I missed Ruben more and more as I saw him less and less. Working in the mine left little time for anything else. When Sunday came around, it took the whole day to rest up and get ready for the next week. Occasionally, I'd see Ruben on the road to the mine delivering props or hauling coal. I was always glad to see him and he was happy to see me, too. I don't know if he missed me as much as I missed him, but I do know he was happy that I was doing well and getting paid well for my work. Eventually I lost touch with him and never saw or heard from him again after I left Pennsylvania. I've wished a million times I knew what happened to him. I'll always wonder if he ever knew how he changed my life.

Chapter 3
Uncle Sam Wants You

Daddy finally found his way out of that dead-end life and joined the Army along with his five best buddies: Lynn Mayberry, "Hut" Chappell, brothers Bill and Clarence (aka Cotsey) Keilman, and Bill Moffett. That was 1940, just before the United States became part of World War II. Serving in the First Infantry – the Big Red One – he and the Keilman brothers were stationed together and fought side by side in North Africa. At Oron, North Africa, Cotsey was seriously wounded; getting him off the battlefield and to safety became Daddy's main objective. As Cotsey was being treated by the medics and evacuated from the area, accompanied by his brother, Daddy questioned if he would ever see his dear friend again. But the luxury of wondering was short lived; there was still a war to fight to the finish.

It was many years later when Cotsey telephoned Daddy one night. Daddy was so glad to talk to him and was obviously moved by the call. He didn't say much about it to any of us children; like most of his other life experiences; he kept those thoughts to himself. We had heard him speak of his buddy Cotsey, though. All we ever knew about him was that he and Daddy were very close childhood friends. Later, we learned that Cotsey's injuries on the battlefield had left him confined to a wheelchair. What stirred Daddy's emotions was the fact that Cotsey told him that he knew his life had been saved by Daddy pulling him to safety when he was wounded; he just wanted to say thank you.

In 1995, the First Infantry Division held their reunion in Orlando, Florida. Although Daddy had never before attended one of the reunions, he learned that Cotsey and his wife Alice were living in Florida. My sister, Cathy, and I began making plans and within a week's time we had all the arrangements for Daddy and Momma, the two of us and our spouses to go to Orlando. While Daddy spent some special time with his comrades, especially Cotsey, we enjoyed a trip to Epcot. At the banquet on Saturday night it was so exciting to actually meet Cotsey and see how he and Daddy interacted with each other. You could easily tell they were still very good friends in spite of being separated by miles and years. It seemed to me like I had known the Keilmans all my life.

Our assigned seating was almost front and center of the dais. Cotsey mentioned that he was usually pretty nervous in a situation like this, a large room full of people and him in the middle and not near an exit. He explained to me that he preferred being close to a door in case of an emergency. I told him that he need not fret about that. If there were any kind of emergency, Daddy would be sure that he and everybody else got out of there safely. Cotsey then leaned over and put his hand on top of mine. He smiled and said, "LeeAnne, nobody in the world knows that better than me." There is no description for the pride I felt inside just then, realizing that my hero was Cotsey's hero, too.

As Cotsey's health began to fail, he and Alice moved to Michigan to be near their son, but he and Daddy kept in touch. They always spoke on the anniversary date of some event related to World War II. I don't know if it was the date of Cotsey's injuries or the date of a particular battle. When

Cotsey passed away in early 2002, it broke Daddy's heart, and left him the lone survivor of the six buddies who joined up together.

Chapter 4
"The Big Red One"

From late 1942 until late April 1943, German Field Marshall Rommel and General Omar Bradley engaged their respective troops in some ferocious combat on the desert of North Africa. Thousands of soldiers died and thousands more were taken captive as those battles raged. Following the initial invasion of North Africa, the Allied Forces took a real beating. Many of the Americans had just arrived to fight actual combat after months of simulated training in England and Scotland.

Rommel's Panzer tanks and elite fighting force known as Hitler's SS troops had the definite upper hand in those early weeks of fighting. Both the American and British forces suffered tremendous losses. But the ability of the Allied commanders to quickly assess the overall condition of the battlefield, re-think previously made plans, give authority to junior officers in the field to make on the spot decisions, and then execute all those changes during the heat of battle brought a turning point in favor of the good guys.

The Battle of Kasserine Pass in February 1943 might have been the first major battle in that area. The eight days of intense fighting from start to finish almost mimics a compressed version of the entire North African conflict.

Two groups of Allied soldiers, one an artillery unit and the other a corp of engineers, first entered Kasserine Pass to prepare explosives and lay a mine field. As they completed their work and readied themselves to rejoin the waiting division for the planned assault, they were surprised to find themselves suddenly caught in a well laid Nazi trap.

The two advanced units were totally unprepared for combat as the German troops began to fire. They were unable to escape and had no weapons other than small arms to defend their positions against the full force of the German 5th Army and 10th SS Panzer division. Casualties were heavy and the situation did not look good at all for the Allies. Finally, though, the American Army's First Infantry Division was able to reinforce the pinned down units and Allied air power was able to dominate causing Rommel to retreat for the moment.

The American First Infantry Division, often referred to as "Yanks" by the other forces, came into these battles pretty green, fresh off the training grounds. But the Fighting First or "The Big Red One", as they came to be known, proved to be the source of great pride and confidence for commanders such as Maj. Gen. Terry Allen, Gen. Omar Bradley, and Gen. George Patton. Battles like Kasserine Pass left as many as 6,200 soldiers dead in the North African desert. By the end of April 1943, following 115 days of continuous combat, the Germans surrendered over 200,000 soldiers to the Allied Forces.

The war in North Africa was an experience no survivor would ever forget, regardless which side you defended. The fighting was brutal and vicious; anyone who survived was just thankful to be alive. Daddy was one of those survivors and moved on to Sicily to continue the triumph over evil. The German soldiers that were taken captive that day were fortunate to have lived through it, and unbeknownst to them at the time, they were fortunate that the red haired Sgt.

Marlett – affectionately called "THE Big Red One" by us – lived through it too.

Chapter 5
POW Camp Opelika

In June 1944 Sgt. Marlett was sent back to the good ol' USA. His life was suddenly quite different than it had been just a few short weeks earlier. He had not even speculated about this part of his life since as a young infantryman, he knew the chances of returning stateside alive were minimal at best. But on July 4, 1944 he reported for his next assignment: POW Camp Opelika, located in East Central Alabama.

He arrived by Greyhound bus along with eight or ten other soldiers from various parts of the country. He saw right away that this part of the world was as foreign to him as any place he had seen overseas. The pace of life was slow, the locals spoke English, but it sure sounded strange compared to the English spoken in Pennsylvania. Cotton was growing right up out of the ground along with lots of other crops. It definitely did not look like the desert land he left in North Africa, but it certainly seemed just as hot!

People often question why the POW camps were set up stateside instead of prisoners being held in facilities where they were captured. The answer is basically logistics; air travel and food preservation was not as sophisticated in the 1940s as it is today. It was much more economical to transport the prisoners here to provide the kind of care that was given them during their captivity and at the end of the war transport them back to their homeland. Had the prisons been located overseas, food, clothing, medical care, and enormous amounts of other supplies would have had to be sent over continuously.

When Daddy arrived in Opelika, most the camp personnel were off duty to celebrate Independence Day. So Daddy planned to get his barracks assignment, unpack his gear, and spend some time in the mess hall getting acquainted with whoever might show up. In general, he hoped to just rest up before starting work.

His plans changed in a flash when the CQ came into the mess hall to ask for volunteers to join a search party. Had a prisoner already escaped!? No, they were organizing with local residents to look for an elderly gentleman who had wandered away from his home. Daddy and some other volunteers searched the thick woods until darkness made it impossible to continue. The next day he and the chaplain's assistant still did not have duty orders, so they volunteered to rejoin the search.

The old man, now known to them as Mr. Slappy, was said by his family to have left with his two dogs and they would most likely still be together. They were pretty sure the dogs would not leave his side. It sounded like it would make finding them easier since the dogs would probably bark at anyone coming near.

The search ended later that day when Mr. Slappy's body was found, his two loyal dogs seemingly standing guard over him. They were just fifty yards from where Daddy and his search partner had been when the search was suspended the night before. Daddy has questioned many times since then, if Mr. Slappey's body had been there the night before, why didn't the dogs bark? I think probably Mr. Slappey was alive and on the move at the time they had been there.

I know Daddy's infantry training included the ability to appear out of nowhere when least expected – at least he was able to do that when I was a kid! But I know under those circumstances he would not have been that quiet.

Daddy spent several weeks as Sergeant of the Guard. Late at night, when the camp was quiet and still, he would often talk to the camp and local telephone operators. They all soon became very good friends; one of the operators brought her sisters to a dance at the camp one night. The red haired sergeant and the camp operator's sister fell in love and married on January 30,1945. They rented a small house just across the road from the main guard gate.

When it was discovered from his 201 file that he had been in combat in North Africa, he was assigned to the 3rd Compound at Camp Opelika. His responsibility was to guard the German SS troops who had been captured in those battles like Kasserine Pass. On the surface this turn of events could look really bad for the POWs, but they soon would learn why they were so fortunate that "the red-haired American" had been among those who had survived there.

The 3rd Company consisted of Divisions 9-12, each housing 250 prisoners. Daddy was promoted to the rank of 1st Sergeant in the 11th Division. Being the decent man he is, he was determined to do his job and, surprisingly, felt no animosity toward the prisoners. He understood that they were engaged in combat in North Africa fighting to defend their country, just as he had been. They were all soldiers, all human beings, and would be treated with respect and dignity based on that. The mandates outlined in the Geneva Convention would be strictly adhered to.

Military protocol is an important part of discipline to Daddy, even today. He still believes strongly that military uniforms should be starched, pants bloused, pockets buttoned and brass and boots polished to a shine. I find it hard to understand why as kids we got such a kick out of standing around in a circle taking turns spitting on his boots as he polished them. Even if we didn't comprehend the fascination of the process, we definitely understood the importance of the spit shine!

Sgt. Marlett was not so unique in this way of thinking. Col. Cronander, the Camp Commander, was often the guest speaker at local civic organizations. The treatment of the prisoners was an issue that he discussed over and over with the local residents.

Observing the personal interactions between the prisoners and guards, one might forget that just a short time before they had been equal enemies, determined to kill each other. I believe the structural organization of the camp itself was conducive to a smooth transition.

There were two German soldiers who spoke English assigned to assist Sgt. Marlett. One was a first sergeant and his responsibilities were basically the same as Daddy's: managing the division regarding issues of discipline and work assignments. He reported directly to Daddy, who, in like manner, reported to his captain. The other assistant was the company clerk and handled all the personal correspondence for the prisoners. The clerk reported to the German first sergeant. This type of organization made the day-to-day operations of the camp flow much more smoothly than they would have without such a gap being bridged.

One who never had the opportunity to be on the receiving end of Daddy's personable nature would probably view his relationships with the prisoners as something ranging from strange to unsafe fraternization. However, the mutual respect they had for one another went a long way toward maintaining order. It appeared that the prisoners were reconciled to their captivity and determined to make the best of it. Generally speaking, they were very disciplined and proud. Not the pridefulness you associate with arrogance, but the kind that makes one respect himself and those around him.

Insubordination was rare because the prisoners held themselves accountable to each other. I believe this is a virtue essential to coping with captivity. That is not to imply that life for POWs or their guards was easy or fun. It's just where they were at that particular point in time when the world was at war.

Not everyone was as co-operative as most. There was a German private who was somewhat defiant and insisted on wearing his full German military uniform, even though it was prohibited. He had been warned by the German first sergeant not to wear it again or he would face disciplinary action. He chose to disregard that order and, just as his own first sergeant promised, he was disciplined by his own, and never caused any more trouble.

Formation was required twice a day for roll call for the 250 prisoners in each division. One morning at formation, there were only 248 heads in the 11th Division, no matter how many times they were counted. It was quickly reported to head-quarters that there were two POWs absent from camp. A community alert with their descriptions was sent out. The next morning at roll call, there were 250 men in formation for the 11th Division. Daddy reported to the captain that all prisoners were present and accounted for. The two "escapees" were taken into the orderly room and questioned as to how they had escaped and why, where they had gone, and, particularly, how they returned.

I don't know the details other than they never really wanted to escape. They just wanted to see what the camp looked like from outside the fence. They went about fifty yards outside the perimeter, climbed a tree and stayed there all day watching the workings of the camp all out of curiosity rather than a desire to escape.

Wars, in general were obviously fought by different rules than they are today. Probably the fact that the "escapees" were confined here in the States rather than in war zones familiar to their homeland had much to do with what transpired that day.

As some soldiers were talking one day in the mess hall, Daddy recognized a familiar sound - the "Yankee talk" he had heard all his life. He could actually understand what was being said. Daddy joined in the conversation and learned this guy was also a sergeant, worked in the salvage shop and was, indeed, from the same area of Pennsylvania Daddy called home. Needless to say, they became good friends sharing common bonds, one of which was a desire to organize a ball team.

It was not long before the ball was rolling, so to speak. The company clerk posted a notice on the bulletin board and in short order they had put together a pretty good softball team. Col. Cronander authorized the use of a 2½ ton truck and driver from the motor pool. After duty hours they could travel to other towns nearby to play teams in the same league.

One night Daddy slid into second base hard enough to separate the bag from its pin. He was safe at second but he suffered a nasty cut on his knee. Without the secured base in place, he slid across the exposed metal pipe protruding from the ground. He and his teammates cleaned the gash as best they could so he could finish the game. When they returned to camp that night he went to the infirmary where it was properly cleaned and bandaged. As far as Daddy was concerned, it was history. It had only take one good hit to tear it open, so in his mind two good cleanings and bandages should have taken care of it. (He still thinks like that!)

After a couple of days he was unable to continue ignoring the terrible pain. He told his German aides what had happened and they insisted he let their medic look at it. To his surprise, but to no one else's, he had a raging infection in the wounded knee. The German medic treated it and told him to keep it wrapped in red flannel cloth until it was well. He did as instructed and it healed up beautifully; the knee never gave him any trouble. Had he followed the instructions given him the first night it was treated, it might have healed as well, but to him that German medic saved his leg and got him back in the line-up. He was enormously grateful.

Daddy began to see the German medic as his personal physician and they liked each other. The medic had become quite fluent in English and told Daddy he had been an artist in civilian life prior to the war. One day as they engaged in casual conversation, the medic said he would like to paint a picture of Daddy. The next time Daddy was in the nearby college town of Auburn, he took a list of supplies the doctor would need and purchased them. The medic was thrilled to get them and a few weeks later presented his new friend with a gorgeous oil portrait of Momma and Daddy. Using a photograph kept on Daddy's desk as a model; he had painted it on a piece of tent canvas then put it into a frame hand-made from a dismantled orange crate. Today, 60 years later, that portrait is as beautiful as ever; it hangs in my home as one of my most prized possessions.

Vacations were something unheard of if you were a soldier at that time. But in August 1944, a master sergeant in the records department at Camp Opelika discovered from Daddy's file that Daddy had never had any basic training. When he had enlisted late in 1940 it was not a requirement; there was a war to fight and soldiers were needed overseas at that point. So in 1944, after four years of military service, two of them in overseas infantry, Sgt. Marlett was off to boot camp!

He reported to his new company commander. While waiting in the outer office for his presence to be made known, he heard a booming voice from the inner office. "Marlett! What in the h— are you doing here?" He didn't know exactly how to respond until he entered the office and discovered the commanding officer had been his platoon leader in Sicily. The two of them had a wonderful time visiting, reminiscing, and catching up until Daddy had to report back to work at Camp Opelika. Vacation was over.

One can't help but appreciate the extraordinary talents and creativity of the prisoners. As the good rapport Daddy had with them became even better, they taught him to play chess. One of them hand-carved a magnificent chess set out of red and white cedar and gave it to Daddy as a gift. Individual community members donated musical instruments and the prisoners organized a 32-piece orchestra. In the evenings nearby residents would sit in their yards to listen to them play.

They also had a theater group whose actors and support members brought elaborate productions to the stage, along with some follies productions as well.

Education was considered an important accomplishment and the prisoners who had not completed their studies were encouraged to do so. There were also opportunities for anyone wishing to continue classes aimed toward higher degrees. Over 7,000 POWs enrolled in classes to study American democracy and collectively spent about $12,000 of their own earnings to buy books for the class. Their earnings were derived from wages paid for working on nearby farms.

As they were working the fields one day, some of the prisoners spotted an abandoned collie pup. It was against regulations for them to have an animal inside the compound so they asked Daddy to take him. The puppy was named Jerry and a platform was made for Daddy's bicycle so Jerry could ride back and forth from work each day. Jerry became a great companion and was known at the USO for drinking as much beer as most other soldiers.

While out on a work detail another day, a couple of prisoners found a beehive and brought it back to the camp.

They tended it faithfully and it produced a lot of good honey for them. When they were transferred to another camp they were not able to take the beehive with them. They wanted to give it to Daddy and, although he appreciated the gesture, he told them to give it to one of their friends. He explained that he didn't know how to take care of bees. The prisoners assured him the bees would take care of themselves and then added, "And you are our friend." How could he say no to that?

Chapter 6
Home-run King

Opelika, Alabama was and still is a small southern town compared to most. Although the area has grown tremendously over the last twenty years, there is still so much old southern charm and tradition there. It's a place where recreation league softball is a summertime activity enjoyed by entire families. Ours was no different. Daddy usually played right field, and some times as a centerfielder. There was no elaborate sports complex as seen in many municipalities today; just two ball diamonds joined somewhere around center field. But some really great softball games were played on those two fields. I was told that Daddy once played center field for two teams on opposite diamonds at the same time. I realize now that this was an exaggeration or somebody's vivid imagination, or that they learned I was about the most gullible kid in town!

One fact which was never disputed by anyone was that Red Marlett was probably the best home-run hitter in the league. When he was on deck to bat, all the kids who were playing in the red mud would run to the hillside that provided the backdrop for the fields. Most often when at bat, Daddy would plant the ball onto the bank of that hill.

Whoever could chase the ball down and turn it in at the concession stand got a free Coke.

Many times teams would play double headers or a team scheduled for the second game would not have enough players, so Daddy would stay to play with them. It never really mattered what the reason was for staying at the ball field. The fact was, we were staying. One of our family traditions was to run the bases after the games were over and before the bases were taken up. The rules were simple... Daddy and one of us would both start at home plate and race around the base lines. Daddy ran counter-clockwise while we dashed to first base turning for second, streaking for third base and racing for home plate. Sliding was not allowed. We thought it was because Daddy might trip over us knowing it would be a close race, but we would get there first. Actually, it was because we already had enough red dirt on us and didn't really need to take home any more. The runner crossing home plate first won. You must remember that there were at least four of us kids there on any given night and Daddy had often played two complete ball games after working all day. But he faithfully raced each one of us individually. The kids always won since Daddy would stumble, fall, or pretend to pull up lame. I suspected that he usually let us win, but that might not have been the case. I didn't realize it then, but now I see that the man does get tired some times!

We would stop for ice cream cones on the way home and while traveling the last mile home, my little brother, Rusty, and I would often fall asleep in the car. After all the physical activity he had engaged in from working all day to playing all night, he would then have to carry us in the house and put us to bed. Momma would come in and wash us off as much as possible. Our little bodies seemed to bring home half of that red dirt bank where we ran down the home-run balls.

Daddy was thirty-seven years old when Rusty was born. After all us kids were adults, Rusty also played softball, usually with a church league. The only reason I mention this is to put into perspective the good physical condition Daddy remains in. For several years, he and Rusty played on the same team. Daddy was almost sixty-three years old when he began wearing trifocal glasses. He finally hung up his bat and glove after that. He said it was just too dangerous to play in the outfield and have to decide in a split second which ball to catch since with those new glasses he saw three of them coming at him at one time!

Chapter 7
Telephone Man

Daddy was known around town as The Telephone Man since he worked for the phone company. In the years prior to fiber optics, cell phone towers, and the internet, the phone company was Southern Bell; my daddy was a PBX installer/ repairman. That meant he spent much of his work day up on a telephone pole, which was totally amazing to me. I thought he could climb straight up a pole just like a monkey. Not being the most observant kid in the neighborhood, I never really noticed that he strapped large metal spikes on the bottom of his boots and had a safety harness looped around his waist. It would not have mattered to me because, again, he was "the man" – big, strong, smart, knew everything and everybody. It was nothing out of the ordinary to me that he should also be able to shimmy up a pole.

We had numerous ancient artifacts around our house, like blue, green and clear insulators from the cross arms atop the poles. Our picnic table was a cable reel about five feet in diameter mounted onto a cut-off telephone pole. Perhaps it was the other end of the pole which held up our mailbox. We even had an old telephone booth right behind our back porch. There was no service to it, but it sure did prompt a lot of conversation. In my mind, Daddy was actually Superman and that was his home booth base!

Another big part of his job was talking to our elementary school class each year about telephones and how they work. What a glorious day it was when my turn came for "show and tell" and I took Daddy as my exhibit. I never really knew exactly what a PBX installer/repairman did except, of course, install and repair PBXs. But I was absolutely positive that Daddy was the only one of them and no phone anywhere would work unless he put it in.

There was at least one disadvantage to being reared by such an important communications worker. As we got older we began taking advantage of the phone by talking to our friends for hours at a time during the summer. This was way before call-waiting and not many things irritated Daddy more than calling home to check on us during the day only to hear a busy signal over and over and over again. Attached to his tool belt was a piece of equipment known as a "test set;" it was a telephone receiver with no telephone attached. He could plug that thing into something while he was perched up there at the top of a pole and actually create what is known today as a three-way call. Technology had not made such capability available to the residential customer at that time. When his voice cut in saying, "This is your daddy; get of that phone!" our friends would ask "what was that?" Our response was always the same, "I gotta go." Click. He taught us early that the phone line is not secure for private conversation. No kidding!!

One day in the mid-1960s, though, life for the telephone man changed forever. Racial unrest was quite an issue in the south. I believe that racial prejudice is something children learn by osmosis, absorbed much in the same way a child learns language. It did not seem out of the ordinary to me to see "Whites Only" signs posted in café windows, public restrooms,

On the front of the water fountain in the Montgomery Fair Store, and even on the mechanical horse we could ride for five cents. This was not the kind of mechanical horse made popular a few years ago by the movie "Urban Cowboy". It did not simulate a bucking bronco. Its movements were more like a rocking chair with a saddle.

Being a "white only" kid, I was unaffected by any of this; I paid very little attention to what was happening within sixty miles of home. The Civil Rights Movement was in full swing, George Wallace had made his stand in Tuscaloosa blocking the door at the University of Alabama to prevent Vivian Malone and James Hood from registering for classes. The march from Selma to Montgomery made the evening news. Many protest marches in and around Tuskegee had stirred conversation among many of my parents' friends.

The VA Hospital in Tuskegee had one of those PBX things and something was wrong with it. As usual, The Telephone Man went to fix it. But as the day unfolded, Daddy's workday became very unusual. He had no way of knowing what tragedy had occurred the night before in that town. An altercation between a black male customer and a white male gas station attendant resulted in the white man shooting and killing the black man. By mid-morning the news of the incident was widespread and the racial tension was pretty volatile. A large group of angry black men had gathered in town, and as the hostility escalated due to the phenomenon known as mob mentality, revenge became the common goal.

When break time came, The Telephone Man got into his company truck and headed into town to get a cup of coffee. He had been having trouble with the truck's transmission so he had it out of gear as he rounded the corner coasting toward the town square. His telephone truck was an old van with double doors on the back which were unlocked at the time. Daddy must have looked like a sacrificial lamb to that mob. To this day I've never heard him describe in detail what happened other than to know that Divine Intervention saved his life when the van was suddenly swarmed by the mob. They jumped on top of the van and began to rock it from side to side attempting to turn it over. With rope in hand they intended to pull him out and get the justice they deemed was in order for the death of the customer the night before.

Miraculously they never tried to open the back doors. Daddy was suddenly able to see a clear path in front of him and shifted that old van into first gear. Then he sped out of town as fast as he could go leaving his tools and work orders at the VA hospital. He drove to Auburn and I'm not sure what he did for the remainder of the workday, but he did not tell anyone what had happened to him.

However, within days he was no longer the big, strong man I knew. He was withdrawn and sick, unapproachable, unresponsive, and I was frightened. Such things as nervous breakdowns were not discussed openly at the time, particularly in the presence of children. It was a condition not readily accepted by an employer, either. Daddy's work partner, Tom Oscar, ran a lot of interference for our family during those difficult days. For weeks and weeks it seemed like Daddy just hid in the bedroom. Our family physician would make house calls to see him, but to me, Daddy was gone.

One morning as we were getting ready for school, there was a knock at the back door. When Momma answered the door, there stood an elderly black man; face to face they were both quite apprehensive. Finally the man asked if this was where Mr. Red lived. Hesitantly Momma told him it was and he told her that he worked at the VA Hospital in Tuskegee. He just wanted to tell Daddy that he was sorry about what had happened to him.

It was months before Daddy was able to return to work. Deep inside he was still strong, but he didn't feel it and I couldn't see it. It took a long time, but he was able to come back from that horrifying experience. I wish I knew who the old gentleman was who came by that morning. I believe the courage it took for him to come to our house and contact Daddy might have re-lit the spark that began to restore Daddy's confidence and bring him back from the brink. Fortunately, today, as a family, we do not harbor resentment toward anyone individually or generally for that difficult time in our lives.

Chapter 8
Summer Camp Crises

Like so many soldiers, at the end of the war Daddy joined the National Guard. His desire to protect and defend our way of life did not diminish when the active fighting was over and there was no longer a need for so many active duty servicemen.

Some of the earliest memories of my life are events related to Daddy's military service. Nearly all the people I knew outside our neighborhood as a child (since I didn't get out much on my own) were the families of men who were also members of the Alabama National Guard

For two weeks every summer, the National Guard units went off to summer camp. It was a time Daddy always looked forward to and Momma dreaded. It seemed like a crisis of some sort would always arise while the men were gone those two weeks. Following are some of my most vivid memories of those summer camp crises.

A FISH TALE

Daddy kept a large pond in our backyard stocked with bass and bream; it was situated about a hundred feet from our back door. Our house was not air conditioned so the windows were raised in the spring of the year and not lowered until late fall. We were lulled to sleep every night by a symphony of croaking sounds from some of the biggest bullfrogs in the south.

Disaster struck one year during summer camp when the water level in the pond began to decrease at a fairly rapid rate. The pond was fed by underground springs and ordinarily the amount of rainfall or lack of it had no real effect on it one way or another. However, in just a few days the pond became a huge mud hole. Some of the larger bass were still full of spirit and tried to swim through the mud. But there were so many of them and so little water that their backs looked like shark fins sticking up out of the thick mucky water. It was obvious to all the neighbors that if the rest of the water disappeared and nobody helped those poor fish, the entire neighborhood was soon going to be overtaken by a stench so foul it would be unbearable.

People began showing up with hip boots, hose pipes, and any kind of container that would hold water. Most of the older teenage boys from the community spent an entire day down in the sludge, sometimes as deep as their mid thighs. Keeping a keen eye watch for water moccasins, the boys would catch those fish bare handed. They would have to throw them backwards over their heads onto the bank because they couldn't turn around bogged down in the mud. As the traumatized fish hit the ground, they were scooped up by us little kids and taken to a triage station manned by some of the adults. They were separated into two groups: survivors and casualties. The casualties were buried in a large, unmarked mass grave; survivors were transported back to volunteer neighbors' homes in the various containers brought to the scene. They were then placed in holding tanks such as #2 wash tubs, children's wading pools, buckets, and in the case of a couple of enormously dedicated families, their bathtubs. There they stayed in foster care until Daddy could get home and take care of the breach in the dam, get the water level back up in the pond and return the lucky aquatic creatures to their homes.

It's really not possible to express appreciation to friends and neighbors for such unselfish sacrifice. Although the threat of impending stink might have been the motivating factor for so much help, the big neighborhood fish fry that summer hosted by our family seemed adequate thanks.

A TWIN CRISIS

I married at age 17 and two years later gave birth to a fine set of twin boys. It was six weeks before their due date and, of course, Daddy was away at summer camp. Jason Andrew, 4 pounds 10 ounces, and Daniel Walker, 5 pounds 1 ounce, arrived good and strong early on a Tuesday morning in June 1974.

Momma placed a call to Camp Shelby, Mississippi and, amazingly, Daddy was quickly located on post. When informed that he had a call from home, he feared this would be a crisis to top them all. Personal calls to summer camp were very much out of the ordinary. The sound of Momma's strained voice turned his worry into panic. The stress of the long hours of waiting outside the delivery room had set in and after saying the twins were born early, she began to sob uncontrollably. He couldn't tell if she was sharing good news or bad news! It was several minutes before she could tell him that the babies and I were fine. When he finished his work for the day, he drove the 200 miles home to see for himself and brought two sets of enlistment papers!

Just three years later my third baby boy was born. Daddy was not away at summer camp then, but he probably wished he were by the time Barton Joseph and I came home from the hospital. As with my first delivery, the labor lasted an extremely long time, and Daddy was tapped for babysitting duty with the almost three year old twins. Always resourceful, he found a way to keep the boys from running away from him in different directions while they played outside. He tied one end of a 100 foot rope around the waist of one toddler, the other end around the waist of the other toddler and with a white knuckle grip, he held onto the middle of that rope.

Today, all three of those boys easily recall numerous hours spent with their Pappy as some of the most enjoyable times of their lives.

"BUTT, GENERAL, SIR..."

There was a time when the health hazards associated with cigarette smoking were not widely known. Smoking was common and socially acceptable then. Many people rolled their own cigarettes and most commercially produced brands were manufactured without filters. But as society changed and issues such as preserving the environment were discussed more and more, attention also turned toward the health risks of smoking. Tobacco companies answered the call by promoting filtered cigarettes. The practice of discarding the finished smoke onto the ground had, up until then, been of no great consequence. But as the filtered cigarettes gained popularity, the ground soon became littered with the discards that were no longer biodegradable. Daddy had also routinely discarded his finished cigarettes on the ground, but now he was concerned with how unsightly it made the landscape.

His duties as first sergeant included maintaining strong discipline in the ranks; he still insists that a neat appearance directly reflects a high level of discipline. He routinely removed cigarette filters from the ground and deposited them into the "butt cans" located throughout the camp. This practice was of his own personal volition and not an issue involving the military unit as a whole.

That is until the day when the two became intertwined with another issue that did involve the unit. Instead of dropping handfuls of cigarette butts into the cans, Daddy began to hold back a few, making sure he always had access to some of them. He was adamant that anyone in uniform must keep his shirt pockets buttoned. If they didn't, he would fill the open pocket with those nasty butts.

One thing you can always count on is that Daddy will do what he says he will do unless there is a good reason not to – such as the laws of physics make it impossible. When asked what he would do if he saw a general with unbuttoned pockets, he reminded the men that a proper uniform was a matter of discipline and the general had not achieved his rank by being a sloppy, undisciplined soldier.

Camp Stewart, Georgia was the site for National Guard battery units throughout the southeast to continue training at summer camp. On Saturday morning there was a planned General Inspection; the battalion was in formation at the arrival of the adjutant general. The Opelika unit, B Battery, was third in order for inspection and they were ready. The soldiers looked sharp, the tanks were washed, and if Army green could shine, those tanks would have. There was no lack of pride among these men; their anticipation was great.

As the general made his way down the line of Second Battery, he came into the line of sight of Sgt Marlett and the Battery Commander. As they watched him complete his inspection of C Battery, they noticed him unbutton his shirt pocket, remove his sunglasses from inside and put them on. At that moment someone distracted him, they spoke, he returned a salute and moved on from C Battery to B Battery. The flap of his unbuttoned shirt pocket was as plain to see as were the ribbons that also adorned his chest. They both stood out to everyone present except the general himself.

Inspection protocol dictates that the battalion commander step up, salute the general, and introduce the battery commander to him. The battery commander follows suit by stepping up, saluting, and introducing the first sergeant. The first sergeant would then step up and salute; the general would return his salute and shake hands with them, then conduct the inspection. The formality is quite impressive to soldier and civilian alike and in a perfect world, there is no deviation from this ceremony.

But in a perfect world there would never have been a dilemma as big as the one facing the red headed sergeant right then. His peripheral vision allowed him to see at least eight enlisted men standing on a tank watching him closely as the introductions were made. It was obvious everyone was wondering what he would do about that unbuttoned pocket screaming at them from the general's chest. The world around him seemed to stand still then spin out of control when the moment approached and the pressure was on. Daddy was introduced, stepped up, saluted, and said, "General, the uniform dress code states that shirt pockets are to be buttoned and seeing that yours is not, with the general's permission, sir, I will button it for you." And he dropped the cigarette butts into the open pocket, buttoned it, stepped back and saluted.

At this point, both the battalion commander and battery commander wanted to disappear. The only response from the general was a very subtle change in his facial expression, but it was not possible to discern its meaning. The general returned Daddy's salute and continued with the inspection without any further incident or flap (no pun intended.) Sgt. Marlett was reflecting on how proud he had been of his first sergeant stripes and what they meant to him, since he was pretty certain that this would be the last day he would wear them.

As the general departed the battery area, he turned, saluted the men and said, "Keep up the good work." As soon as possible the commander demanded an explanation. It was doubtful that the general's departing comment had been directed at Sgt. Marlett. Daddy explained that the only thing that was for sure was that he had done what he felt he had to do in order to maintain the respect of his troops. He had told them what would happen under such circumstances and this was no time for backing down. It would have meant losing the confidence of the entire unit. The commander said he would wait and see what the battalion commander would recommend regarding the incident.

Later that evening at the officer's meeting, the general's aide and another officer were casually discussing the events of the day. The subject of the first sergeant who had reprimanded the general soon came up. Another officer chided that the sergeant was probably a private again by now. At that point the general joined the conversation saying, "He better not be demoted for that."

That was the end of the discussion on the matter until the following morning when the general was riding past the parade ground. As he approached B battery, he had his driver stop. He got out of the jeep and walked directly over to Sgt. Marlett saying that he just wanted to check to see if the sergeant's pockets were buttoned. Except for the informal discussions immediately following the incident, and those that continue to surface until this day, nothing else was ever said about it as far as disciplinary action. Sgt. Marlett retained his stripes and respect of his men. Just another day at the office?!?! Maybe.

THE LAST SUMMER CAMP

The summer of 1981 was met with both sadness and excitement for Daddy. It would be his last summer camp with the Alabama National Guard. Even though he would have liked for us to believe it had always been two weeks of grueling, intense training, he viewed it as an exercise similar to what we know today as a paintball Saturday that stretched into fourteen days. He looked forward to it with great expectations.

All the paperwork for active duty was in order and the months of preparation complete, down to the last detail. Except, of course, the one that could never be managed ahead of time. What semi-catastrophic event would take place this year to divide his attention between Army and civilian life?

As the scheduled dates neared, it was clear that the crisis this year would not occur at home while he was away. It would be his constant, unwelcome companion for the entire two weeks. He had developed a severe case of shingles and was in excruciating pain with it even before he left for camp.

Momma strongly encouraged him to forgo camp that year. She suggested that perhaps it was God's way of allowing him to just be able to reflect on the wonderful years he had enjoyed in the past. But he could see nothing good or divine about that plan. Besides, what if the unit was to be called upon to single-handedly defend the country and was forced to perform their duties without him? Unthinkable! With the same mindset of General Patton as he described the hardships soldiers of his generation had endured, Daddy's reaction was, "call in sick because of a virus? NEVER!!"

So off he went to fight a simulated war for the last time, enduring pain that he would try to imagine was the result of a battlefield wound. That would at least make it more bearable, and also make the training exercise more realistic.

But, it was not to be as he had planned. He reported to camp and remained there for the entire two weeks. But he was unable to participate in the planned exercises. As the virus ran its course, the pain associated with it seemed to peak during that two-week period. He was forced to spend his days at the camp headquarters rather than in the field.

It was impossible for anyone to know the depth of despair this caused him. It was obvious that he was disappointed, but I believe he also entertained some feelings of self loathing. For the first time in his forty one years of military service, he was physically unable to perform his duties. The aura of excitement that had surrounded him in years past was not there at this home coming. In those days the families of the guardsmen would gather at the armory on the afternoon of the unit's scheduled return. There was so much excitement and anticipation as the wives exchanged stories with each other and the children played. All the time every ear was on alert for the sound of the blaring horns of the jeeps and trucks as they entered the city limits and announced the convoy's approach. We had always been fascinated hearing his first-hand accounts of the camp experiences. In an official capacity, the stories were called "after-action reports" but, sadly, this year there would be none other than how miserable Daddy had been.

But true to form, rather than ever admit defeat, especially to a virus, Daddy had a plan. He requested permission to attend another camp later in the summer with another guard unit. By then he would be over this temporary setback, ready to report for duty and hit the ground running. How his spirits soared when he learned permission was granted. He was ready to take on the world and rid it of every foe all by himself. But he would have to wait until all the details were sorted out and his orders were processed before he knew when to begin this enormous undertaking.

He was confident now that his last camp would indeed be a good one. While waiting for his official orders, Daddy and Momma took some time off to drive to Ohio and Pennsylvania to visit relatives. Anxious to know that every detail was covered, he called me from my uncle's house with instructions to contact headquarters regarding his orders. He wanted to know if they have been processed and whether he needed to do any thing other than wait for them. Waiting was, and still is, a difficult task for him. I was to let him know as soon as I had any information. Actually, he was already in his "military mode" and said, "report back to me ASAP."

After several phone calls, I was finally connected to someone who knew about the arrangements in question. As I waited on hold listening to the Armed Forces public service announcements programmed on the telephone, I wondered if Daddy installed that, too. Suddenly the recorded voice was interrupted by a live, booming voice that said, "Sgt. Marlett!" Apparently, the officer at the other end of the line was under the mistaken impression that Daddy was calling. When my meek and slightly intimated voice answered, "Uh, no Sir, this is LeeAnne, his daughter," he yelled into the phone, "Where is that rascal?" Without hesitation, I replied, "Cleveland, Ohio...Sir."

He laughed hard and asked how he could help me. I told him that Daddy had asked me check on his orders and let him know the dates to report to camp. The officer then told me why he had tried to sound so big and bad when he took my call. After forty-one years of exemplary service to Uncle Sam, Sgt. Maj. George J. (Red) Marlett was AWOL! The unit had reported two days earlier and Daddy's orders had arrived in the mail the day after he and Momma left for Ohio. My brain went into overload... Oh my goodness, what have I done? Daddy's AWOL, the MPs must be looking for him, and I just told somebody in the adjutant general's office where to find him. They're probably en route already to pick him up. He's going to spend the rest of his life in the brig and we're all going to have to move to Ft. Leavenworth, Kansas! And the worst part of all is that I'm the one who has to call him back and break the news!

My life could not get any worse right then, but I soon came to my senses and asked the officer – who was still laughing – what I should do. He pulled himself under control and said, "You don't need to do anything else; you've been a big help and the MPs will take it from here." Again he just seemed to explode in a fit of laughter as I was immediately convinced that my previous assessment of the situation had been accurate. It looked really, really bad.

Sensing that I was not amused, he apologized for pulling my leg and said he just was not able to resist the joke. He sure wished it had been Daddy that had called instead of me. He got one more laugh at my expense when I responded, "Yes, sir, me, too!"

He went on to assure me it was really not a problem. The orders had been processed late and Daddy's current status would be changed from "absent from duty" to "pending notification of duty." They would assign him to another unit and he could report with them the last two weeks of August. We both laughed then although my heart was not as filled with merriment as his appeared to be. All he had left to do was get the paperwork in order. I still had to report back to the Sarge! At least there were nine hundred miles between us and when the conversation ended, I could just hang up the phone. Momma and a large portion of the population in Cleveland, Ohio would hear about it for days.

Everything played out beautifully for Daddy, though. His new orders were processed just as promised and he spent his last summer camp filling the role of first sergeant, instead of the E-9 rank he currently held. This was perfect in his mind; he often said his most enjoyable years in the military were when he served as first shirt.

FORCED RETIREMENT

On November 17, 1981 George J. Marlett turned sixty years old, but to him it was no time for celebration. He received notice that due to his age he would have no choice but retire from the military he had loved and served so well for four decades. It didn't matter that he could complete the fitness course in the time allotted and do so ahead of some of his superior officers and NCOs many years younger than he.

Daddy was furious that the bar had been lowered and a portion of the required mile-and-a-half run could now be completed by *walking*. Why is it called a mile-and-a-half <u>run</u> if you're not expected to <u>run</u> it! To make matters even worse, the course could be done with shirt tails out of fatigue pants and pants legs out of combat boots! To him these standards, or rather lack of standards, encouraged serious breakdowns in discipline and were totally unacceptable.

Since the Department of the Army did not share his views on this matter, his mandatory separation from active service was probably a good thing for all involved. It was highly unlikely that he would ever concede his objections and agree with them. I can't think of many situations which would have frustrated him more than continuing to serve under compromised guidelines that he had always considered to be offenses subject to disciplinary action.

So on November 30, 1981 wearing his dress uniform and looking as dashing as ever, SGM George J. (Red) Marlett smartly saluted his commanding officer for the last time. He did so with the same patriotic pride he felt forty-one years earlier when he saluted his CO for the first time.

Momma and Daddy continued to call Opelika, Alabama home and lived there until she died just three months before their 58th wedding anniversary. One month following her death Daddy was invited to unveil a historical marker commemorating POW Camp Opelika. It was placed at the former site of the main gate to the camp, just yards away from where he and his beloved wife had shared their first home. The day was filled with mixed emotions: the sadness of a void which could have only been filled by the presence of Momma, the excitement of friends and the pride of four generations of his family being in attendance, some who had traveled great distances to share in this day. Daddy looked so sharp wearing the same dress uniform he had worn when he was discharged from the military twenty-two years earlier.

A great soldier once said, "Old soldiers never die, they just fade away." It was decided by all of us children that Gen. MacArthur's statement was absolutely right. I've informed my siblings that whichever one of us is the last one left, please make arrangements for someone to look out for Daddy and keep him out of trouble because he will no doubt still be going strong!

Chapter 9
Family Convoy Confusion

Deer season brought great excitement to the male members of our family. Every year they planned a hunting weekend on my cousin's farm about eighty-five miles north of Opelika. Though the actual hunt and camping were for just the guys, the planning and preparation involved the whole family. Several weeks prior to the opening of deer season, we would all converge on Hoyt Lee's farm to spend the day visiting and enjoying each other's company while clearing trails in the woods and re-enforcing old deer stands. As our sons became old enough to participate in the hunt, their anticipation and excitement would build as each laid claim to "his spot" and new deer stands were erected. Once the trails were cleared and all stands determined safe, each hunter would pick out the place in the barn where he would camp the weekend of the big hunt. (Why sleep outside when there was a perfectly good barn to sleep in?!)

At the end of the day we feasted on good ol' southern barbecue or enjoyed a fish fry and relaxed in the satisfaction of a job well done. All too soon it was time to head for home.

One year the crowd included Momma and Daddy, of course, my brother Rusty and his family, my sister Pat and her family, and me and my family. Obviously we traveled in more than one vehicle since some had to come in pick-up trucks to bring tools and lumber.

Times have changed a lot since I was a little girl. We had not come as far as the widespread use of cell phones. When more than one vehicle traveled together, communication between vehicles was a challenge. We would use whatever was necessary to get the attention of the other traveler. More often than not we used scraps of paper to make signs that read GAS or BATHROOM. Anything much more involved than that required you to stop and discuss the problem. Those occasions were reserved for things pretty extreme like car trouble or "did you get my tool box off the porch?" or your head-count had come up short from what you had on the way up. Sometimes a kid would decide he wanted to ride with Granny and Pappy. This was fine, but we needed to know who was where.

This caution on my part stemmed from an incident when I was eight years old. Our huge extended family had gathered in Tallassee at Aunt Annie Lee's for Christmas. Around mid-afternoon while I was in the bathroom, I realized the house had become extremely quiet. I was fairly certain I had been left behind and for some reason was afraid for anyone to know it. So I stayed in the bathroom until I could figure out what to do.

Fortunately, my Aunt Myrline had forgotten a casserole dish and had returned to get it. When I heard her voice, I bolted out of the bathroom, saying nothing to anybody as I sprinted for her car. It didn't matter to me that the car was already filled with my aunt, uncle, cousins Dawn and Joy, their boxer bulldogs Duke and Duchess, plus the baskets used to carry food to the reunion. They lived in Columbus, Georgia and I knew they would go through Opelika to get home. On most occasions like this, with or without a stowaway, they would make a pit stop at our house; I planned to just get out there when they stopped. So I climbed into the third seat of their station wagon squeezing between the dogs and ignoring the laughter and comments about how lucky I was they had come back. I was just relieved to know I would be home before New Year's.

About ten miles down the road we saw our car pulled off the road waiting for Uncle Bob and Aunt Myrline to pull in behind them. As we did, Momma got out of the car and asked, "Is LeeAnne with y'all?" Oh, an all too common question. The details would change, the name would change, but the situation was always the same: headcount had come up short! There were so many of us it wasn't hard to lose track of at least one kid. As we grew up, married and had children of our own, it didn't get any easier. It just added to the confusion.

However, on this particular trip home from the farm, the need to stop was not an emergency as grave as a child missing in action. But it was urgent since one of them had to go to the bathroom. Since it was after dark and impossible to read the BATHROOM sign, the next best thing was flashing headlights. With Momma and Daddy in the lead truck, us behind them, Rusty and family following me, and Pat with her family bringing up the rear, I flashed my lights at Daddy to let him know I would be stopping. Since I didn't do anything else to indicate trouble, they would know it was no emergency, just a routine pit stop, the kind you make when you travel with kids.

At that time, Highway 280 was the main route between Opelika and Birmingham and heavily traveled. It was still two lanes most of the way and ran through several small towns. That part of our state is quite hilly. Perhaps that is the reason the two vehicles behind me saw my flashing headlights and knew I would soon make an unscheduled stop. However, unbeknownst to me or anyone else, Daddy had not been able to tell the difference in my flashing lights and the reflections made when driving the hilly terrain at night.

As they came into town, Rusty and Pat turned off to go their own respective ways. I had built a house in the woods on the family property and lived less than a quarter mile behind Momma and Daddy. My boys and I thoroughly enjoyed our peace and solitude there. Daddy constantly worried about my safety since mine was the only house back there in the woods. When they pulled into their driveway and began unloading his truck, he realized for the first time that I had not come in right behind him.

After our pit stop the boys had fallen asleep and I decided to travel the back roads home to take advantage of the quietness. All was right with my world until I got home and noticed Daddy's truck was gone. In semi-panic mode I pulled into their driveway to investigate. The house lights were on and things he brought back from the farm were unloaded on the carport. No longer expecting anything terribly wrong, I left my car running and went inside to see what was going on.

As soon as I opened the back door Momma came into the kitchen with the strangest look on her face. I asked where Daddy was and she said, "He's gone to look for you! What happened?" When I explained my unscheduled stop, she began questioning when? Where? Why didn't I let them know? I told her I had flashed my headlights for about a mile before stopping and that Pat and Rusty both flashed theirs at me as they passed in a gesture of "see you later." She took a few deep breaths and calmed down. Our attention now turned toward poor, panicked Daddy back-tracking Highway 280 looking for me. I was sure he would drive all the way back to Hoyt Lee's looking to meet us coming home or find us on the side of the road. I felt really bad about my decision to take the back county road home.

By this point, my boys were fully awake so I turned off my car and brought them inside. We called Rusty and Pat to see if either of them had heard from Daddy. Rusty assessed the situation right away and just said, "Oh, h— sister, you are in big trouble!" All we could do was wait for Daddy to give up the one-man search and come home to organize a search party. Momma made a pot of coffee and we waited.

Every moment that passed made me more anxious than the one before. I knew if Daddy left in a panic to look for me, by the time he gave up finding us and came home he would be nearly hysterical. I was absolutely right. An hour and forty-five minutes later he burst through the back door looking and sounding like the first sergeant I had known all my life. "Where have you been? What was so important that made you break formation? You know that you never, NEVER, **NEVER** just drop out of a convoy!" I decided my best defense was to just apologize and go home, leaving it up to poor Momma to calm him down and explain. She could call Pat and Rusty to report "situation under control."

From that day on, two vehicles traveling together would have walkie-talkies or some way to communicate... especially if one of them was mine.

The first weekend of hunting season finally came and all the guys arrived at the farm with their gear. The weather was good. It was cold, perfect for deer hunting. They started to settle in for the night, showing off new rifles or scopes and swapping the same stories they had heard the year before but enjoying them all over again. Daddy looked over at Bart's bed roll and could hardly contain himself when he saw that it included an electric blanket and enough extension cord to power it from home if he had to! Daddy really kidded him about it and told him hunters need to be able to rough it. Well, Bart got a new story to tell the next few years when Daddy left camp late that night in search of some more quilts and a kerosene heater!

LESSON LEARNED

Cathy, my sister just older than me, had not been home in a long time. Her husband Mike was a career Air Force officer and they usually lived far away. It had worked out that Cathy and one of her daughters, me and my three sons, and Momma and Daddy had the opportunity to go to Vogel State Park in Blairsville, Georgia for a weekend in the mountains. The boys and I had been there numerous times; we were all looking forward to it.

Daddy would never consider such a trip into parts unknown unless the route was marked clearly with a highlighter on an atlas map. So just a couple of months following the convoy fiasco, all the usual pre-planning sessions were complete. Rest areas along the way were noted in case we got separated; we still didn't have the communication thing between vehicles completely under control!

Friday afternoon came and we loaded Daddy's truck with firewood, blankets, boxes of dry-good groceries, and coolers. Foods like spaghetti and chili were cooked ahead of time and placed in coolers, under the misconception that we were going to relax, not cook! Some people take a lifetime to learn that in order to eat, someone has to cook!

Cathy and I piled into my car with our children. We had our marked map, went over our planned route "one more time" and Daddy said, "Lil Anne, take us to the mountains." Nobody said a word as I pulled out ahead of him and he followed along right behind me. I think it was the first time I had ever seen Daddy in my rearview mirror...actually, I'm sure of it!

About fifty miles from home Cathy finally couldn't stand this blatant violation of standard operating procedure and just blurted out, "Why is Daddy letting you lead?" I glanced at her and said, "He's not; I'm just driving in front." She looked so bewildered I went ahead to offer the explanation before she even asked for it. "Ever since the night I dropped out of the convoy, I have to drive in front of him so he can keep an eye on me. He really is leading. If you watch closely, you'll notice I don't change lanes until his blinker comes on. If I drive too fast he'll get so far behind me that somebody might get between us, so I have to slow down to his speed. If he has to speed up to stay with me, then I would think it was okay to go faster."

She understood perfectly well that illogical reasoning. It's one of those things you inherently understand but can never explain. It was a wonderful, fun and relaxing weekend, although we did cook a little bit.

Chapter 10
Learning from Example

The year 1991 brought a major change to the direction of my life. As I said I was single again, my children were now fine young men. I had a successful career and enjoyed living just behind Momma and Daddy. It had been understood by all of us children for many years that I would assume the responsibility of caring for our parents in their golden age. Things were falling right into place to allow me to easily step into that role with little difficulty.

Thirty years earlier I had seen first hand what an honor it was to be the one chosen for such a task. In spite of her inability to take care of him when he was a child, Daddy built a house across the pond from us for his mother when she retired. For the last twenty-six years of her life, Momma and Daddy provided everything Grandma needed to maintain a comfortable life.

Just like me, Momma had also been the fourth of five children and in the 1980's she gladly became the primary care giver to her widowed mother who was an invalid. Without any hesitation or reservation, Momma and Daddy moved Mama into their home and tended to her every need for the last five years of her life. Although I saw Momma quite frustrated and near exhaustion both physically and emotionally at times, I knew she would not have traded those arrangements for anything in the world. I learned so much from watching her care for her mother and I hoped that when the time came, I would be able to rise the occasion with the same kind of tender patience and gentleness.

For me, life was looking good. I was confident that my three sons would be successful and productive adults, my parents were enjoying good health and a full, active life. Momma still missed her mother a lot, but she often commented on how thankful she was that God trusted her enough to let her raise her own children and still be able to care for her mother. I know just how she felt!

Chapter 11
In-law or Outlaw?

In March 1993, out of nowhere it seemed, Bobby Evans, my dear childhood friend since first grade, reappeared. We had grown up in the same neighborhood; he had younger and older siblings who were classmates with my siblings. Bobby, too, was single again and totally committed to raising his six-year old son, Matthew. He was Matt's custodial parent and a good daddy; they were great buddies.

Bobby and I had known each other for nearly thirty years as friends who could be trusted. Since we had so many things in common, it was easy for us to reconnect at this point in our lives. We were both single, self-sufficient, hard working and not at all interested in romantic relationships since we both knew how complicated they could be.

Going out to eat together or just watching television was a much needed distraction from the daily grind we both had created for ourselves. We enjoyed each other's company and laughed a lot about occasions in the distant past. Like the time in second grade when our class was playing Red Rover. Another classmate and I called, "Red Rover, Red Rover, send Bobby right over." He looked like a mad bull charging us and as he braced himself to break through our tightly clinched hands, we panicked and let go of each other. He ran right through the line without the expected resistance, stumbled on the soft air, fell hard and broke his arm. In a round-about way I guess you could say it was our fault, but my goodness...what's a girl to do!

Through the summer of 1993 Bobby, Matt and I spent more and more time together and easily fell crazy in love with each other. Matt was a blessing I never expected to have. I had always wanted four sons; but judging from my long labors, I was not built for delivering babies easily. I had decided I would only have another child if someone gave him to me. And that's just what God did.

Bobby and Daddy became great friends with an enormous love and respect for each other. In the barn Daddy kept an old Coke machine he had rigged to dispense ice cold beer for 45¢. He shared with Bobby the secret of how to use the same quarter and two dimes to get a brew. A few close mutual friends were privy to the machine, but by invitation only and none of them shared the secret. When Momma and I would scold them about cheating the machine, they would say, "Well, we've already paid for that beer once." No argument from me on that issue.

One day they were enjoying one of their bull sessions in the barn where they often spent hours tinkering with tractors and sharing a brew. Their conversation got around to our relationship. Bobby assured Daddy that me and my well being were fast becoming very important to him. It was obvious that I was so happy to have another little boy and it appeared that Matt loved me. Daddy certainly approved of our relationship and I think he and Momma knew Bobby and I would get married before I did.

Knowing the task that lay ahead of me, I was determined there could be no one in my life who might interfere with my commitment to my parents. Bobby was just as conscious of the years he had ahead of him bringing up his young son. According to Bobby, my willingness to care for Momma and Daddy at home was one of the things he loved about me.

At our 20th High School Class reunion in August, Bobby announced to our classmates that we were going to be married. When Labor Day weekend came, we both had a few days vacation. Matt was spending time with his mother, so we decided to go to New Orleans for the holiday. Knowing that such a thing would be frowned upon by both our families – respectable unmarried members of the opposite sex should not make overnight trips together – we stopped by the Lee County Courthouse on our way out of town and got married. I knew I had married a wonderful man, but I never could have imagined how great it would be, or that anyone other than Daddy could ever rise to the status of hero in my life.

Chapter 12
Medical Mayhem

As the 90s moved on, Momma's health failed and she became chronically ill with diabetes and complications from a bout of hepatitis. By 1995 she was suffering from liver disease and rapidly losing her eyesight to macular degeneration. More and more she became dependent on me for just day to day help even though I was still working full time. I would come home from work, fix supper and make two plates to take up to Momma and Daddy. While they ate, I would gather their laundry, sort their mail and pay bills, and tidy things up a little. By the time I got back home Bobby and Matt would have already eaten and settled into their evening routines.

I began to worry that Bobby might feel some resentment about how much time I spent away from home. It was common for Momma or Daddy to call me to come back to their house for one thing or another before the night was over. I was also the emergency contact person at work so the police would call me whenever they found anything unusual when making security rounds after hours. I would then have to go the office and secure the building. Sometimes I would stay a while and take advantage of the opportunity to catch up on some paperwork for a couple of hours without interruptions.

After a few years at this pace, Bobby feared that I would be overcome by stress and would self-destruct. He would point out to me from time to time that he was worried about me. But I would defensively respond that he knew what he had signed on for beforehand. I didn't realize that he was not complaining at all, but was genuinely concerned for me.

As the century began drawing to a close, life became pretty rough. It was a really cold winter; Momma had confined herself to home and did very little for herself any more. The Y2K threat loomed from every venue claiming our high tech lives would come to a screeching halt as we passed into the new millennium. We prepared for such a scenario much like everyone else by stocking up on non-perishable foods, medicines, bottled water and stashing some cash in a safe place at home.

Christmas was quiet that year. Momma and Daddy were anxious about my three older sisters traveling home for the holidays since Y2K might cause travelers to get stranded. Daddy didn't feel very festive anyway. He had a bad cold and couldn't seem to get over it. His regular physician was in the process of retiring and only saw patients in his office, no longer at the hospital. It appeared Daddy was getting worse no matter what we did to help him. In case he needed to be admitted to the hospital for treatment, I took him to another doctor.

Having never seen Daddy before, the doctor tried to gently remind me that Daddy was seventy-eight years old and not a strong, young man any more. I was finally able to convince him that this seventy-eight year old was a strong, OLD man who works circles around the rest of us on a regular basis.

He worked as a volunteer at the hospital three times a week, and normally was the first to arrive at the gym every morning before daybreak for a full hour-long workout.

A flu/pneumonia epidemic was in full swing all across the country that winter. If there were any possible way to keep sick people out of the hospital, it was best since the germs there were claiming lives every day. The doctor prescribed medication for Daddy to take at home, but said if he did not improve within twenty-four hours, he would have to admit him to the hospital. I kept a pretty close watch on him for the next several hours. He finally drifted off to sleep in his recliner. He seemed comfortable with less fever than he had had in several days.

About mid-afternoon, my brother Rusty came out to deer hunt behind my house. I walked down to our house to tell Bobby and Matt so they would not go out to the woods. I found a note there from Bobby that he and Matt had gone to eat Chinese food, something they both enjoy a lot and I do not. How unusual it was to be alone in a quiet house. I was about to treat myself to a bubble bath when the phone rang. Thankfully I was still dressed because Momma was frantically saying, "I need you; Daddy can't breathe."

I knew we were heading to the emergency room so I went to the back yard to fire a three-shot distress signal for Rusty. If Daddy was as weak as I expected him to be, I would not be able to get him out to the car by myself.

When I came into their house a minute later, Daddy was leaning across the dining room table coughing and wheezing with every shallow breath. I realized there was no time for an ambulance and that Momma was so frightened she would need someone with her. So I decided to start toward the door with Daddy knowing Rusty would probably be at the back doorsteps before I got there. Trying to support Daddy's six foot, 205 pound frame on my scrawny little 115 pound frame, I said, "Daddy, let's start making our way to the car.

You need to go to the hospital." He turned his glazed eyes to me and said, "Not (*cough*) now (*wheeze*). Some (*cough, wheeze*) thing is wr- (*cough, cough*) -ong with (*wheeze*) Rus- (*cough, wheeze, wheeze*) -ty."

Startled, I asked Momma, "What's happened to Rusty?" She replied, "We don't know; we heard three shots from the woods." So relieved, I said, "That wasn't Rusty's distress signal; it was mine!" Daddy gasped, "(*cough*) What's (*wheeze*) wrong (*cough, wheeze*) with (*cough, wheeze, wheeze*) you? (*cough, wheeze, gasp, cough)"*

"YOU ARE, DADDY! YOU'RE SICK!!!" I yelled just as Rusty rushed through the door. He helped me get Daddy to the car, and then stayed to comfort Momma. Man! What excitement.

I called the doctor from my cell phone; he called the emergency room and made arrangements for a direct admit. I was so glad to hand that big sick man off to a strong, male nursing assistant with a wheel chair. He took Daddy to the medical floor, set him up in a VIP suite (one of the benefits provided for hospital auxiliary volunteers) and I took care of the administrative details. By the time I completed the forms, Rusty had joined me. Bobby and Matt were staying with Momma who was anxious to hear word of Daddy's condition.

Daddy's bad cold had quickly spiraled down to a full blown case of pneumonia; it would take some really aggressive treatment in the hospital to bring him through. We tried to navigate Momma through the corridors without exposing her to too many bad bugs so she could be with Daddy, in spite of the fact that he was growing some pretty bad ones himself. But with her at his side, he began to improve. There was a lot of discussion about whether or not taking her there was a good idea. Rusty and I knew, though, they would both cope with this crisis much better if they were together.

After several days Daddy was discharged to recuperate at home. It appeared that he had "dodged that bullet." He remarked to us that he really thought he was near death. Bobby, Rusty, Momma, and I never said it aloud, but I think we all felt the same way. Little did we know that two days later he would relapse and go through this all over again, only worse. He was admitted again through the ER, same floor, and same suite as before. But as New Year's Eve approached, he became pretty depressed since he was not responding to treatment.

In all their fifty-five years of marriage, Momma and Daddy had never spent New Year's Eve apart. With the possible Y2K problems looming in everyone's minds, the hospital administrator had arranged for patients in house on New Year's Eve to have one family member spend the night with them. The suite was large and comfortable with soft chairs and a love seat that made into a full-size bed. We made plans to bring Momma to the hospital late in the day, but before dark to avoid any inebriated celebrators, so they could be together for the night.

I enjoyed being able to spend the evening at home with Bobby. Neither of us has ever spent New Year's Eve out celebrating; it's just not our style. As a matter of fact, Bobby was usually in bed asleep by 9:00 o'clock every night, but that's too early for me. That night was no exception, so I went back to the hospital about 10:30 to check on the folks. Momma and Daddy were sitting side by side on the love seat, the television tuned to the Bill Gaither Family New Year's Eve concert. They were holding hands, both of them with heads way back, mouths opened, SOUND ASLEEP! It was so funny to me; I laughed out loud and woke them up. They laughed too and I knew our lives would soon return to its normal chaos.

Chapter 13
Mi Casa Es Su Casa

Early into the new century, Bobby and I agreed that taking care of two households and working full time was too much for me. It would certainly be easier if we all lived together. But, personally, I've never known any house to be big enough for two women–especially if one of them is me! Our two-story home with upstairs bedrooms would absolutely not accommodate us all. There was also Matt to consider; fourteen-year-old boys have very specific needs and sharing a bathroom with grandparents sure does not fit well into that mix.

Momma and Daddy's house was spacious, but the floor plan did not lend itself to a workable arrangement either.

According to God's perfect plan, there was a house on five acres of land inside the city limits and less than a mile from the hospital. I'm not sure a home could have been custom-built that would have suited our needs any better. It was a beautiful brick home situated about two hundred feet from the highway with a circle drive winding through a nicely landscaped yard with large shade trees all around. Originally it had three bedrooms, two baths, a large living room, separate dining room, large eat-in kitchen with an extra large walk-in pantry and utility room. It had been vacant for about eighteen months and was listed for sale at a reduced price.

The current owner had been a caterer and had converted the enclosed garage into a commercial kitchen. She also added a large bathroom and huge banquet room bringing the total floor space to about 4000 square feet. There were already separate heating and cooling systems and septic tanks in place. But now that she was going out of business, all the appliances had been removed from the kitchen and it was just a large empty space. Neither side of the house had an entire kitchen of its own which is likely the reason it had not sold.

Bobby and I walked all through the place, commenting on its size and pointing out all the possibilities it held for housing two families...in particular, one elderly couple and one mid-40ish couple with a teenage son. Daddy and Bobby are both excellent carpenters and I am not exactly a stranger to paint, wallpaper, hammers, nails and saws myself. Besides how many times do you get the opportunity to buy a house and design the kitchen exactly the way you want it?

We decided to present the idea to the folks, took them to see the house and they agreed it was possible. Daddy was not quite as willing to take such a step as Momma was. So we talked about it some more. A couple of weeks later when Cathy and Mike came to visit, we mentioned it to them. They thought it was a great idea, and we all talked about it some more.

The house was laid out in such a way that we could easily all live there without getting in each other's way. There was plenty of space for privacy and a good spot for a large vegetable garden. We could both sell our houses for more than enough money to pay cash for this one. I would be able to retire and devote as much time as needed to Momma. Matt would have plenty of privacy and there would still be plenty of room for all of us to sleep when all five children came home to visit.

Daddy was still holding out though. Cathy asked why he was so hesitant since it appeared to be the perfect set up. He finally confessed that he had never felt old in his entire life until we started talking about this move. It had never crossed his mind that any of us would ever think that he couldn't take care of Momma. Well, honestly, it had never crossed our minds that he would even think that we thought that was the situation.

In the sweet, reassuring spirit that she is so gifted with, Cathy persuaded Daddy to see the big picture. Momma's health was bad; she had diabetes, liver disease, basically blind, and had also developed a bleeding gastric ulcer. It was obvious that she would soon need 24-hour care. While we were all confident of his ability and willingness to give it, if he and I shared the time and energy it would take, we could both do it better. Boy! She's good!

He agreed. Matt liked the plan. And Momma knew within herself what was ahead. Our offer on the house, contingent on the sale of our homes, was accepted and our house sold within a week of being listed. Arrangements were made for us to go ahead with the deal even though Momma and Daddy's house was not even listed on the real estate market yet.

It was going to take a heck of a lot of down-sizing to combine our two households. This was particularly true since we were all pretty sure Momma had not discarded so much as a plastic bag in many years! At a strategy meeting one night we began discussing what to keep, sell, or give away. We were looking at the duplication of numerous appliances and furniture. The keep part was easy for Momma, but the give away and sell list proved itself to be an obstacle of gargantuous proportion to her. Finally, exasperated, she asked me, "LeeAnne, where are we going to put all this stuff?" When I replied, "Well, Momma, all of it is not going with us," it took her by total surprise. She exclaimed, "What do you mean?" I told her that the plan was to get rid of a lot of it. In a voice becoming shriller with each word, she said, "Like what?"

This was a bad, bad sign. She was having some serious second thoughts and "Cathy, the Calmer" wasn't here to explain things. I looked around for something useless, or at least unimportant, and saw a collection of old telephone books dating back nearly twenty years. I pointed to them, blew off some dust that covered the top one, and said, "All these out-dated phone books for starters." She glared at me and said, "A lot of the numbers in those books are still good, you know." I took a deep long breath and silently said to myself that this might be a whole lot tougher than I first thought.

Eventually things started to fall into place. Not realizing that Cathy was co-conspirator in a well-laid plan, Momma and Daddy were invited to her house the first weekend in March. While they were gone, Bobby and I began the "great exodus" from Morris Avenue to Waverly Parkway. We rented a U-haul truck, enlisted the help of friends and moved everything necessary for basic housekeeping from both houses to our new home. When Momma and Daddy were ready to leave, Cathy told them to go to their new address.

The purpose of what we did was not at all to be sneaky or devious; rather it was an act of mercy. Cathy and I saw how difficult it was likely to be for Momma to leave her home on the land she had inherited from her parents. The small block house next door had been built for her parents by the loving hands of their children and their spouses almost a half a century earlier. We believed it would be easier on her emotionally if she did not have to re-live moments like the passing of her mother in that bedroom as we broke down her bed and loaded it on the truck. Also, there was the outside chance that she might forget about those phone books if she didn't know exactly where they were.

Chapter 14
A Mind Of Her Own

By June we were all pretty much settled into our new home and things were going well. I had cut my work hours in half and was able to come home on my lunch break each day. One day as we sat on the back patio drinking a glass of tea before I was due back at work, Momma said, "I just can't seem to catch my breath very well." I responded, "Yes, ma'am. It's so hot out here and the humidity so high it makes everybody miserable." But as I watched her more closely, I became convinced that her breathing difficulties were not related to the 95 ° heat or the 70% humidity.

I walked inside to call my office to tell them I needed to take Momma to the doctor. My boss, Dr. Lee, is one of the kindest and most understanding Christian men I've ever worked for when family obligations are concerned. His family comes first to him and it is important to him for his employees to share that same value.

At the doctor's office we learned Momma was experiencing severe congestive heart failure and needed to be treated in the hospital. Daddy met us at the hospital and stayed with Momma while I took care of the paperwork. Since he lived close by Rusty arrived at the hospital right away. I drove home to get gowns and a robe for Momma and make all the necessary phone calls. Our oldest sisters live in different parts of the country; Cathy lived about three hours away. After some discussion with her husband Mike, we decided they would drive in the next morning.

With all the important business taken care of, I gathered Momma's things and the emergency bag I kept for myself and returned to the hospital. I learned then she had been admitted to CCU; her heart rate was dangerously slow, as low as 24 beats a minute. She was on oxygen and a cardiologist had already been in to see her.

The cardiologist told us that Momma's condition was serious and life-threatening and that a pacemaker was necessary as soon as possible. Our thoughts were varying degrees of "why are waiting then?", but she was too compromised at the moment. Subjecting her to general anesthesia posed a much greater risk of not surviving the night. With atropine and a crash cart by her bed they would monitor her every second. We were encouraged to go home and sleep, let them take care of her and if her condition should deteriorate before morning, they would call us and proceed to the operating room.

Reluctantly, we left. Rusty said he would call Pat and Peggy to update them and I called Mike back. Cathy was at choir practice, but he promised to call her and they would call me back. It wasn't long before they assured me they had already thrown clothes in a bag and were on their way. I was glad to know she would be there and that Mike was coming, too. She is my stabilizer and we grow closer to each other every day. That's sort of surprising since we shared so little of ourselves with each other as kids. But, five years is a gigantic age difference between teens.

Momma's condition remained stable through the night and we all gathered at the hospital early the next morning. As they took Momma to surgery we tried to prepare ourselves for the worst and yet comfort Daddy at the same time. After what seemed like an endless wait, the doctor told us the pacemaker was in place and that she had done well. A collective sigh of relief was followed by Daddy's offer to buy us all breakfast in the cafeteria. We didn't hesitate to take him up on that offer and then headed in different directions to call numerous friends and family to share the good news.

I was so surprised when we gathered back in Momma's room. I had not realized in the preceding days how weak she had become until I saw how strong she was now. Her heart was ticking at a steady sixty beats a minute; her color was good, even her appetite improved.

We didn't know it then, but those were to be the last of her good days. By the end of the year her heart disease had progressed forcing a decision to be made. Could she undergo another procedure to place a stint in one of her heart vessels to relieve a significant blockage?

There was a comical phone conversation one night that could actually be classified as a conference call. At home, Momma, Daddy and I were each on extension phones talking with her internist and her cardiologist who were each on extensions at their home. We were discussing the pros and cons of going ahead with this surgery. Momma listened mostly to the cardiologist who obviously felt it was necessary. The internist (his wife) agreed, but not enough to risk what little quality of her life there still was by performing something so invasive.

Her diabetes brought to the table many possible complications by itself. But her liver disease had also progressed rapidly, and her chances for uncontrolled bleeding were great. We all agreed there was no easy answer; to me it looked like a crap shoot at best.

But Momma decided she wanted to go for it. So trusting her to know more about what she was willing to endure than any of us did, the procedure was scheduled for the following week. Again she came through like a trooper, and overall, she felt better for a short while. Several weeks later, however, her condition reached a point where it was almost impossible to treat one ailment without adversely affecting another.

Chapter 15
Heart of Gold

Momma required so much attention that when Daddy complained that his legs hurt during his morning workouts and that he couldn't finish his mile walk without having to stop to rest, I shrugged such statements off as casual conversation. I was surprised, to say the least, when Bobby opened a conversation one afternoon with, "I'm fixing to tell you something that I'm not suppose to. You do what you think you need to with the information."

I could not imagine what I was about to hear. Our relationship is not one that makes it necessary to issue such a disclaimer before you say something. I was astounded when he told me that Daddy had seen a cardiologist and planned to have a heart cath done in just a few days. When he went on to tell me that Daddy intended to have this done without anyone but himself, Rusty, and Bobby knowing about it, I was furious!

As I thought more about it, though, trying to see it with the same kind of logic Daddy has, I understood that it could very well be a situation he saw as a personal attack. This made him more determined than ever to be in control of it. There was no question that his plans would be derailed, but just how to confront the issue without alienating Bobby was not going to be easy.

As it turned out, Bobby was safe because the conversation between Daddy and me quickly became animated. He insisted it was not a big deal and he didn't want all of us worrying about him over nothing. Most of all he wanted everything to be as normal as possible at home so Momma would not find out about it; he didn't want to upset her. We could not come to an agreement on any aspect of this issue, especially when it came to letting my sisters know what was happening. I was really shocked when he looked right at me and said, "LeeAnne, I forbid you to call them."

He and I never did agree although I presented a much better argument for my case than he did. Believing with all my heart that I was right, I found a private place at home where I was sure I wouldn't be disturbed, and dialed Cathy's number. As soon as she answered the phone she knew it was not a "just passing the time of day" call; we had shared one of those earlier in the day. She was instantly anxious about this call. I started out by saying, "I found out something I'm not supposed to know, and I think you need to know it, too. But it's something that you can't find out and do nothing about. So if you have this information, you're gonna be in a tough spot – a partner in crime, so to speak. So, decide whether or not you want to know."

I was sure it would take repeating all that at least once before she had it all processed, but she caught it all on the first pass. "What, or who, is it about?" was all she asked. As soon as I answered, "Daddy," she said, "Tell me."

I told her what I knew and that, so far, I had not handled the situation very well. She assured me that she would drive down and we'd work this out together. I immediately was confident that Daddy would have to just endure the "circus atmosphere" he feared we would create making such a fuss over him. Since there is safety in numbers, and I knew reinforcements were on the way, before the day was over I called Peggy and Pat, too.

Over the next couple of days Daddy finally agreed we could tell Momma, but not until the night before the procedure was to be done. Cathy, with her wisdom and talent for persuasion, was able to help him understand that Momma needed the same amount of time as the rest of us to prepare for this emotionally. She needed time to ponder it all and ask questions. If there were a decision to be made when the test was over, it would be really unfair to expect her to make a good one if she were still in shock about it. Aside from that fact, she would be as mad as a wet hen with all of us for keeping the information from her in the first place. She was not able to do much for herself, but she was still very much able to speak her mind...even if it had to be with a weakened voice. Daddy agreed and Momma was told.

Cathy had been absolutely right, as usual. When the morning came for the heart cath, we converged on the hospital with Momma in tow. We were all relaxed by this time, not afraid or overly worried since Daddy kept himself in great physical condition. Each of us speculated on why he couldn't walk a four-minute mile without having to rest. The fact that he was nearly eighty years old couldn't possibly have anything to do with it!

While Rusty sat with Momma in the waiting room, Cathy and I were in the room with Daddy. The nurse came in to perform the final tasks before Daddy went with her for the actual procedure. She asked, "Are there any questions, or anything I can do to help your family through this?" We all got a good laugh when Cathy and I jokingly asked if they could dip him for fleas and ticks while he was back there.

I guess Daddy's fears came true – it was a circus like atmosphere, but it was so fun. We always make each other laugh when we're all together. That's exactly what we were doing when the doctor came and suggested we go into a private conference room. The diagnosis was that Daddy had four major blockages in his heart arteries; the only choice was to fix all of them or none - have quadruple bypass or do nothing. As the doctor began to explain pros and cons of each option, Rusty just cut right to the chase. He told him we only needed to know about the surgery.

There was no question about what to do, even though the doctor felt compelled to remind us of Daddy's age. We knew it was a factor, but so far the only time age had ever been a real enemy was in 1991. He wanted to rejoin his old National Guard unit and fight in the Gulf War! The doctors who did not know him were concerned about this, though, since the prognosis is more guarded for those his age.

Daddy was awake and we were all in his room when the surgeon came in to talk with all of us. He repeated almost verbatim what the cardiologist had told us earlier. He added, however, "The blockages in these particular vessels can only be treated surgically if you decide to treat them all. A heart attack caused by the disease process at this point would most certainly result in sudden death." When he asked, "any questions," the only one was asked by Daddy himself: "What are we waiting in here for? Let's do this thing now!" We were all sure that the doctors were about to learn why we were so confident that Daddy would bounce right back from this setback.

On the day of surgery we again converged on the hospital, only this time we were joined by extended family members and lots of friends. So many people, in fact, that the auxiliary volunteer on duty opened a large unused waiting room for us and saw to it that anyone who came in looking for us would be ushered to our "private" waiting room. There was an enormous sigh of relief when the surgeon came in to tell us the procedure was complete. He said that it was textbook perfect and uneventful. So much so that he had trouble trying to think of something else to say other than the standard, "fixed it." After a short stay in the hospital and strict orders to not do much of anything for the next six weeks at home, Daddy was on the mend.

He recovered well and entered the cardiac rehab program with great anticipation. He was as ready as we were to get back to business as usual. By the second week he was trying to push the envelop. When his graduation day from cardiac rehab came, we all looked forward to the ceremony where he would be knighted, "King of the Healthy Hearts." We had known all along that Daddy has a heart of gold!

Chapter 16
Westward, Ho!

Daddy recovered well from his heart surgery and Momma had not had any major setbacks in a couple of months. We decided to celebrate by taking a trip. In just a few weeks we put preparations in high gear and on July 2, 2001 loaded the RV, tow car, and Bart's Bronco with supplies. My four sons, Dan, Drew, Bart and Matt, and Drew's dog, Callie, joined me, Momma and Daddy as we headed for Nashville, Tennessee. We spent Independence Day on the General Jackson Riverboat, thoroughly enjoying a wonderful dinner, stage show and magnificent fireworks display on the river. From there we journeyed into the Black Hills of the Dakotas and spent a couple of days at Mount Rushmore.

Continuing westward, we met up with Pat and her family at Yellowstone National Park. They lived in Great Falls, Montana; it's quite a drive from there to Yellowstone, but compared to the almost 3000 miles behind us, it was not too bad. We lingered about five days at the park and when we broke up camp, Momma decided to jump ship and go home with Pat. Plans were made for Cathy to fly to Great Falls the next week, visit with them a few days, then fly back home with Momma. It was a relief to hand Momma off before something happened to her on the road in the vast western wilderness. The further away from home we traveled, the more I worried about her making the trip. But, just like so many times before, she knew just what she wanted. She had missed Pat terribly; Montana is too far from Alabama to visit very often. And she was willing to endure whatever it took to get to her daughter.

We pulled away from the campground in West Yellowstone going in opposite directions. Daddy, the boys, the dog and I went on to the Grand Canyon, visited some relatives in Arizona, traveled into Mexico and discussed visiting the Alamo. But we had been gone almost a month already. There had been some tense moments brought on mostly by the 100° heat with only 12-15% humidity. Nosebleeds and the close quarters shared by six strong-willed people spanning three generations made for excessive stress.

We finished the trip as it was planned. Nobody ever got so mad that they entertained the thought of surrender and caught a bus or plane home. I think by the time we pulled into our driveway, Daddy and I were tempted to grab a handful of each other's red hair and pull it out. But fortunately those disagreements don't hold a place high in our memory banks. We all agree that it was a trip of a life time.

After just a few days at home, the three older boys were already talking about another trip. It was fun, but they'll have to do the next one without me. I wouldn't trade the experience for a million bucks, but it might take something close to that to make me want to do it again any time soon.

Chapter 17
Up in Arms

A few weeks after returning from our trip, Daddy noticed a lesion on his arm and was concerned it might be a tick bite. (The hospital staff didn't fulfill our request to dip him!) When he saw his general practice doctor for a routine follow-up, he showed the lesion to him. The doctor said it was not a tick bite, but an unusual looking mole, both in shape and color. He removed it and none of us gave it another thought until the call came informing him it was melanoma. In no time, it seemed the surgeon was excising a large area surrounding the site of the removed mole. Waiting for the pathology report on the tissue removed seemed like an eternity. But, the good news came that the margins were clear and the cancer had not spread. Dodged another bullet!

About ten days after the sutures were removed, I wandered into the kitchen early one morning where Daddy was sitting at the table reading the paper. "You finished your workout early this morning," I commented. He looked up from the paper and said, "My arm hurts." I replied, "That was a big chunk of arm the doctor took out; I'm not surprised it hurts." His simple response: "the other arm."

It looked awful to me with a large knot high up on his arm and an equally large sunken area just below it. When I asked him what happened, he said he couldn't tell me. I cautiously asked, "You can't tell me because you don't know or because you've done something you're embarrassed about?" The answer was immediately obvious when he looked again at the newspaper and uttered one word, "yep."

Cut logs from a massive oak tree lay in the field behind our house. In spite of just having had surgery, Daddy decided they had to be moved and stacked neatly while waiting to be split into firewood. He devised a system that enabled him, one-armed, to relocate the logs by rolling them most of the way. All was well until one of them began to roll away and he instinctively tried to catch it. He protected his healing arm, but the weight of the log on his other arm proved to be too great and the strain tore his rotator cuff and its tendon.

So far we had established good relationships with the family physician, the cardiologist, and a plastic surgeon. Guess it was time to break in an orthopedic surgeon. Within a couple of days an MRI confirmed the doctor's diagnosis and Daddy was admitted to the hospital to have his rotator cuff repaired. He was miserable and sore for a few days and again returned to rehab for physical therapy.

As he had on numerous other occasions, he amazed his doctors and therapists. Being incredibly fit, he was fully recovered from that ordeal in about three months.

Chapter 18
I'll Be Loving You, Always

As Momma's general health continued to fail and her quality of life slipped into a downward spiral, there was no comfort in the fact that decisions regarding how to approach her care became easier to make. In most cases, the focus was directed on providing comfort care only. Her gallbladder was causing her to have a considerable amount of pain, but having it surgically removed was out of the question.

Physically caring for her seemed to just consume my life, perhaps because she and I both knew that she was very near the end of her life. For reasons unknown to me, we were never able to talk about that. Thankfully Cathy was always able to approach the subject with Momma without either of them being uncomfortable emotionally. Momma depended on my sister for the spiritual support that only Cathy could give. And I depended on her for it, too.

It's no accident that God makes us so unique in what we are able to do well. Cathy and I have laughed numerous times about how hard it was for her to handle Momma's dentures. She would almost gag when she heard the sound the suction makes when the upper denture was loosened. Equally as strong, although it never triggered my gag reflex, was the anxiety I felt as Momma and Cathy discussed such issues as details of Momma's funeral service.

Cathy was spending more and more time in Opelika and I was so grateful for her help. We grew so close to each other during that time. Whenever it was time for her to go home to fulfill obligations there, she never failed to leave the refrigerator and pantry fully stocked with groceries and casseroles in the freezer ready for the oven with minimal preparation required.

We often commented to each other how hard all this must be for Daddy. As Momma slipped further away from us, Daddy tried to keep to his routine. He continued working out every morning at the gym, and then spent the day busy with yard work or tinkering around the house. He was not as talkative, didn't get too far from home, or stay away very long when he did leave.

By March 2002 Momma was having severe tremors which she described as feeling like a full body muscle cramp. The diagnosis of Parkinson's disease was added to the host of other diseases ravaging her body. This was more than she was willing to battle; it was obvious she was giving up.

We celebrated Momma's 80th birthday on October 7, 2002. As was his normal routine, Daddy helped Momma get settled in her wheelchair at the table for supper on the evening of October 11th. He reached across the table and moved her fingers gently over a small gold angel pin he was holding. He told her, "Momma, this is a little gold angel. I'm gonna pin it on your housecoat so she can look out for you when I'm not here." Rusty and I were both so moved by the tenderness "The Big Red One" showed as we watched this precious moment take place. This was the last night Daddy would feed her supper or put her to bed. The next day she slipped easily from this world to the next as Daddy sat next to her, held her hand, and bid goodbye to his soul mate.

Chapter 19
Lending a Helping Hand

Our relatives up north get a real charge out of the way we prepare for the winter season. Actually we do it much the same way they do. We bring in potted plants, cover outdoor spigots, and make sure there is enough fire wood stacked. The major difference in such routine things is that we start planning to do them around mid-December.

We are often still mowing grass every week and wearing shorts and t-shirts at that time of year. It's not unusual to encourage the family's spirit of Christmas by turning the air conditioning down as low as the thermostat will go and have a roaring blaze in the living room fireplace. The smell of hardwood burning and hearing it pop in there brings comments of peace and contentment from the family gathered in the kitchen. It's too hot to enjoy the fire in the same room, and you can't burn it long or you'll have an outrageously high power bill.

On those rare occasions when snow is in the forecast, our preparations do differ dramatically. Snow does not often come south unless it's accompanied by ice, so we gather the supplies necessary to be at home for the duration. There is usually a run on the grocery stores and discount stores. We stock a least a week's supply of non-perishable foods, batteries, candles, fuel for lanterns and gas for the camp stove and generator.

Our beautiful southern pine trees with their long-reaching branches cannot support the weight of ice. They break and crash to the ground taking with them the utility lines leaving many homes and businesses without power. Hence the need for lamps and generators. Since a crisis of such magnitude usually lasts for several days, you don't use the generator to replace all the power in the house. It's designated for the freezers and coolers in the barn to save the fresh venison you just put there and the frozen vegetables you spent half the summer sweating to preserve. You spend those days shut in, relaxing by the fire in the living room, eating sandwiches and making coffee on the camp stove.

As soon as the storm passes cleanup begins with the roar of chainsaws cutting those pine limbs to a manageable length. They are then relocated from the yard to the roadside. Eventually the city maintenance workers will dispose of them with a wood chipper. Of course, that doesn't happen until all the electric service is restored; that often can take up to a week.

Before he retired from the telephone company, Daddy was one of the men who worked endlessly restoring communication service for everybody. Once that mission was accomplished, he would be busy helping neighbors clean their yards, checking on shut-ins to be sure they had everything they needed. He spent the first twenty years of his life where snow and ice are normal and only the most severe weather would cause such chaos and destruction. He was able to drive on the roads that most southern people deemed impassable.

I believe that even if he had not been confident with his ability to navigate the roadways, he would have traveled by riding lawn mower if need be to check on friends and relatives. Today you can know he will still do what he can to be sure everyone around him is safe and comfortable. You can always count on him to help out and to do the right thing. That's just who he is. Sometimes he is determined to help someone even if it's not in his best interest to do so. He can still be found most any day mowing someone's grass or providing transportation to the doctor or grocery store.

Just before our family reunion in 2004 he called my brother to bring him his old climbing spikes when he came to the big annual event. When Rusty arrived at the park where our huge extended family was meeting, he came to me and asked, "Do you have any idea what Daddy wanted me to bring his spikes for?" When I told him that Daddy had promised to do some telephone work for someone and needed to climb a pole to do it, Rusty's reaction was the same as mine. You just roll your eyes and shake your head. It will take something bigger than his age to prevent the man from doing what he's already said he would do.

So Rusty reluctantly took the climbing gear to Daddy's truck. We both knew it would not deter Daddy in the least if we said that Rusty had just forgotten the spikes. Daddy would not have hesitated to drive the extra fifty miles to Rusty's house to get them.

Daddy spent the next Saturday at his friend's house, fulfilling the promise he had made. His determination to keep his word, no matter what, is one of the things about him that make us all so proud of him. But it was somewhat comforting after he finished that job to have him return home with no broken bones. Better than that, though, was hearing him say, "I need to get these spikes back to Rusty and then I don't care if I never even see them again. I didn't realize how out of shape I am any more!"

Nobody dared say aloud what we were all thinking, "You're not out of shape, Daddy; you're eighty-three years old for heaven's sake! Not to mention it's been 20+ years since you climbed a pole, plus you had quadruple bypass surgery on your heart only three years ago." That last part would have been answered with something like, "That means I ought to be able to climb a pole without any trouble one time at least once every twenty years anyway!" You'd have to know him to fully understand that kind of logic.

Chapter 20
A Son's Perspective

In the summer of 2004 Daddy began to complain of pain and heaviness in his legs. So once again, Rusty, Cathy, and I found ourselves in a hospital waiting room anxious to learn the results of tests to determine the reason for Daddy's discomfort.

It seemed a good time to submit this book for Rusty's approval. He was seated directly across from me. Watching him, I would wonder which section he was reading as he'd smile, chuckle, or allow his eyes to fill with tears that would roll down his handsome face. I found myself relieved to see such emotion, since it confirmed my belief that this is, indeed, a true work of art.

As he came to the last page and looked for more, I was thrilled thinking it was to him like one of those books or movies you get into and don't want it to end. But I was jolted back to reality when he asked, "Where's the chapter about Daddy's battle with colon cancer?" When I answered that I had not planned to cover that particular subject, he told me he thought it was too important to leave out. Since this seemed to mean a lot to him, I asked him to write the chapter and he eagerly agreed. Our sister, "Editor Cathy," gave her okay, and the book we thought was complete, was re-opened...so to speak. The doctor came out and told us that Daddy has peripheral artery disease, but this time, unlike any of the challenges before, he is absolutely not a candidate for surgical intervention. The disease is too severe and it's best to treat it with medication, knowing that it's quite serious and will not get better. Our silence was broken finally by Rusty saying to Cathy and me, "It just doesn't get any easier, does it?" I'm so thankful that my brother was there for Daddy, and for us, too.

After reading his account of that period in the spring of 1986, I agree with my little brother about its importance, and I believe the episode Rusty referred to is best told in his firsthand account.

Being the youngest of five children and the only boy put me in a prestigious position. "Spoiled" would be putting it mildly; my sisters and Momma doted on me. But the fact that I was the only son gave me a very unique bond with Daddy. Two men in a house full of women, we had to watch out for each other. We did things like guarding the bathroom door in the mornings, or making sure the other had hot water for a shower. Simply put, we were buddies.

Our relationship deepened as I grew older, and we began to share many interests. Playing on the same softball team and deer hunting provided hours of quality time for us. Traveling to and from these events gave us the opportunity to hone our skills in another shared passion – Masonic work. Red Marlett is a name known throughout the state of Alabama in Masonic circles. He has forgotten more than most men will ever know! Under his teaching I have been privileged to join the Scottish Rite and the Shrine, both advanced organizations whose first requirement is that you be a mason in good standing. Following Daddy's example, I had no problem meeting that requirement.

Many people say that teenagers don't realize how smart their fathers are until they grow up and become parents themselves. That's just not the case for me; I have always known that my daddy sets the standard. Every passing year increased the level of our trust and confidence in each other.

One Thursday night as we worked side by side cleaning up the Shrine club, Daddy told me a "secret." He said he was having some problems with his bowels but didn't want to tell Momma because she would worry. Then came the shocker: earlier that day when flushing the toilet, he noticed what looked like apple peelings swirling around the bowl. He had finally realized that it was blood.

Momma worrying about him wasn't what he needed to be concerned about at that point. I insisted that he go the very next morning to the doctor. "Don't wait for an appointment; you see him tomorrow!" I was quite adamant about it; obviously my point was well made, since he did go the next day. His family doctor told him that he didn't have time to fool with Daddy's butt hole. (You would just have to know this long-time friend and doctor to appreciate his response to Daddy's complaint.) It was made in the way you say something inappropriate trying to make a joke when confronted with an unpleasant situation. He did, however, refer Daddy to a specialist who performed a colonoscopy early the next week. It revealed our worst fear; Daddy had a tumor about the size of a lemon in his colon.

I was at work when LeeAnne and a family friend came to give me the bad news. I can't explain why, but I felt a peace at that very moment which told me "all will be well; we found it in time."

The doctors gave Daddy the option to go home and ponder his choices. They said to take some time and come back when he had made a decision. In true "Marlett fashion" Daddy let them know he had no intention of taking that thing home with him! He wanted it taken out right then!

They did manage to get him to wait until the next morning. It was decided to remove a twelve-inch section of his colon, six inches on each side of the tumor. They then spliced the two ends together. His ordeal was just beginning however.

Daddy's physical strength was always awe-inspiring to me. I had never seen anything keep him down. Even his bouts with pneumonia were never more than a week or two, and he'd be back, bullet-proof as ever. This time, though, the cure for his cancer almost killed him.

For six months following the surgery, Daddy had to take chemo-therapy. The drug was mixed with orange juice which he would drink on Thursday mornings. By afternoon he would be as weak as a newborn kitten. It would take all the fortitude he had just to move about the house. By the following Wednesday he would have his strength built up again in time for the next dose on Thursday morning.

I had never seen this giant of a man, affectionately known among his National Guard associates as "the Red Rock," get knocked to his knees. But his determination to beat this thing never wavered. After his last treatment it was obvious that not only would he beat it, he would rightfully "kick its butt."

An old Boy Scout proverb says "what doesn't kill you will make you stronger." Daddy did come back stronger than ever. He is a walking testimony that early detection is the answer to treating colon cancer. But I came to realize that year, that my daddy really is just human.

Chapter 21
Editor's Privilege

By Cathy Ponder

If you talk secretly with any one of Daddy's five children, each would probably say, "I'm his favorite." He has the gift of making everyone, not just his children, feel special. My friends from childhood through adulthood comment on how much they love my daddy.

Though I know he doesn't really have favorites, I have been privileged to spend quality time with him. No matter where in the world my Air Force husband carried me, Momma and Daddy came to visit. Perhaps because our times together during those twenty years were limited, I always made the best of them. We have shared cups of coffee and conversations from Slapout, Alabama to the shores of Galilee.

I had the good fortune to travel for six weeks across the United States and back with Momma and Daddy. One day during that journey the conversation turned to spiritual matters. Daddy and I discussed God's amazing love and how God had protected him throughout his childhood and World War II, even though he had no understanding of Who God was. He explained how after they married, Momma had taught him about God and led him to know Jesus as His personal Savior.

His determination to stay in shape has been an inspiration to most people who have met him. I remarked one day on how thankful I was that he had kept himself in such good condition. His reply are words to live by. He said, "You know God has given me a certain number of years on this ol' earth, then He's gonna take me on to glory. Whenever I borrow somebody's car, or a tool of some kind, I take extra care of it 'cause it's not mine. Well, this body isn't mine; God has just loaned it to me while I'm down here. I'll have a new one when I get to Heaven. Until then He expects me to take extra good care of this one."

What an example to follow!

Epilogue

General Colin Powell, US Army (RET), told the story to an interviewer about the morning of his first day of retirement from the Army. He had planned to sit at the kitchen table, drink his coffee and read the newspaper without any concern for how much time he might spend doing just that. But such a dream ended abruptly when Mrs. Powell informed him of a problem with the garbage disposal expecting him to do something about it. All thru his military career he was confronted with issues that required his immediate attention, but never felt so inadequate in carrying out those duties as that disposal made him.

If Daddy had been a career officer, I'm sure our lives would have been very, very different. My siblings agree when I say I cannot imagine how it might have been, I'm just so glad it was not. We would not have been raised right there next to the fishing pond. I would not know how to paddle an aluminum bass boat without bumping the sides and scaring away the fish. I wouldn't know the fly rod line needs to be waxed, or how easy it is to fall out of the boat if you stand up on the edge to retrieve the lure you cast into the catalpa tree.

We were always proud to get to help Daddy with a "work detail" around our house as we were to share recreational time. I do not want in any way to suggest that

Gen. Powell's career was anything less than Daddy's, just different. Seldom would anyone be called to attend most home maintenance needs since it seemed Daddy could do anything. Consequently I, nor any of my siblings, are hesitant when the situation calls for replacing or repairing whatever might be broken. It doesn't matter if it's a hole knocked in a sheet-rock wall or a problem with a major appliance. Although I'm not always successful at it and am forced to call a plumber or electrician (unless Daddy is here), I'm not afraid to attempt the job before conceding defeat.

Many times friends visiting in our home might notice a major change such as a new kitchen floor or a tiled shower. There have been occasions when a wall has been moved. I have tackled major renovation projects on my own, including making our basement entrance area and adjacent laundry room become one room instead of two, and converting the space into a full kitchen downstairs.

Our Christian faith embraces the belief that as you cherish and maintain your relationship with God the Father, and strive to reflect His image, you continue to grow and learn. This makes the problems you encounter in life much more manageable because of lessons you've learned. That basic principle of life applies to one's spiritual life and some of us are blessed enough to have been taught it by paying attention to our physical father as well. Such is the case here. I love it when someone asks how I learned the skills to do the kind of work I do and I can answer, "Watching my Daddy."

When my focus turned toward completing this writing, I looked forward to having Daddy verify some specific details. One afternoon I sat across the kitchen table from him with a list of questions. I was amazed as he answered each one with the most remarkable recall. He would explain a point further and, unwittingly, open up a whole new avenue of information that needed to be organized, researched and included here. I reminded myself that as long as he's alive and kicking, this book can never really be complete. And, no doubt, long after he's gone, there will still be a story inspired by him.

About the Author

Being the 4th and youngest daughter of Red and Maxine Marlett, the 100th descendant of her maternal great grandfather, the only grandchild named after both maternal grandparents, and the 5th generation of that family to reside in East Central Alabama is plenty to be proud of.

What came from her paternal heritage is thick curly red hair, freckled skin, a stubborn streak and a passion for perfection whenever a task or challenge presents itself.

Printed in the United States
34360LVS00001B/274-291